T0294182

TREKKING THE CATHAR WAY

THE GR367 SENTIER CATHARE IN SOUTHERN FRANCE

TREKKING THE CATHAR WAY

THE GR367 SENTIER CATHARE IN SOUTHERN FRANCE

by Nell Sleet and Luke Smith

JUNIPER HOUSE, MURLEY MOSS,
OXENHOLME ROAD, KENDAL, CUMBRIA LA9 7RL
www.cicerone.co.uk

Printed in Czechia on behalf of Latitude Press Limited on responsibly sourced paper
A catalogue record for this book is available from the British Library.

Route mapping by Lovell Johns www.lovelljohns.com
Contains OpenStreetMap.org data © OpenStreetMap contributors, CC-BY-SA. NASA relief data courtesy of ESRI

The routes of the GR®, PR® and GRP® paths in this guide have been reproduced with the permission of the Fédération Française de la Randonnée Pédestre holder of the exclusive rights of the routes. The names GR®, PR® and GRP® are registered trademarks. © FFRP 2022 for all GR®, PR® and GRP® paths appearing in this work.

All photographs are by the authors unless otherwise stated.

Acknowledgements

In the creation of this book we relied on help from a few sources. We'd first like to thank the people of Languedoc that we met: the friendly tourism officers, hoteliers, hosts and locals. The book is all the better for your tips and insider knowledge.

Thanks also to Cicerone – particularly Siân, Andrea and Georgia – who have guided us with a sureness of hand that has been really appreciated.

Our thanks also go to Alan Mattingly, author of Cicerone's previous edition of the English guide to the Cathar Way. We used his book to walk and research the route ourselves, and his directions and guidance were invaluable in creating this new guide. We hope that in bringing the English guide up to date we will encourage many more people to explore this rich and thought-provoking trail.

Front cover: On the Cathar Way with Aguilar Castle ahead (Stage 2)

CONTENTS

Updates to this Guide

While every effort is made by our authors to ensure the accuracy of guidebooks as they go to print, changes can occur during the lifetime of an edition. This guidebook was researched and written before the COVID-19 pandemic. While we are not aware of any significant changes to routes or facilities at the time of printing, it is likely that the current situation will give rise to more changes than would usually be expected. Any updates that we know of for this guide will be on the Cicerone website (www.cicerone.co.uk/1047/updates), so please check before planning your trip. We also advise that you check information about such things as transport, accommodation and shops locally. Even rights of way can be altered over time.

We are always grateful for information about any discrepancies between a guidebook and the facts on the ground, sent by email to updates@cicerone.co.uk or by post to Cicerone, Juniper House, Murley Moss, Oxenholme Road, Kendal, LA9 7RL.

Register your book: to sign up to receive free updates, special offers and GPX files where available, register your book at www.cicerone.co.uk.

Mountain safety

Every mountain walk has its dangers, and those described in this guidebook are no exception. All who walk or climb in the mountains should recognise this and take responsibility for themselves and their companions along the way. The author and publisher have made every effort to ensure that the information contained in this guide was correct when it went to press, but, except for any liability that cannot be excluded by law, they cannot accept responsibility for any loss, injury or inconvenience sustained by any person using this book.

International distress signal *(emergency only)*
Six blasts on a whistle (and flashes with a torch after dark) spaced evenly for one minute, followed by a minute's pause. Repeat until an answer is received. The response is three signals per minute followed by a minute's pause.

Helicopter rescue
The following signals are used to communicate with a helicopter:

Help needed:
raise both arms
above head to
form a 'Y'

Help not needed:
raise one arm
above head, extend
other arm downward

Emergency telephone numbers
If telephoning from the UK the dialling code is 0033.
PGHM (Peloton de Gendarmerie de Haute Montagne): tel 04 68 04 51 03
Emergency services: tel 112 (mobile phones)

Weather reports
www.meteo.fr

Mountain rescue can be very expensive – be adequately insured.

Note on Mapping

The route maps in this guide are derived from publicly available data, databases and crowd-sourced data. As such they have not been through the detailed checking procedures that would generally be applied to a published map from an official mapping agency. However, we have reviewed them closely in the light of local knowledge as part of the preparation of this guide.

ROUTE SUMMARY TABLE

Stage	Start	Finish	Distance	Ascent	Descent	Time	Page
Port-la-Nouvelle to Cucugnan							
1	Port-la-Nouvelle	Durban-Corbières	27.5km	710m	620m	7hr	30
2	Durban-Corbières	Tuchan	27.5km	1000m	930m	8hr	39
3	Tuchan	Cucugnan	18km	790m	650m	5hr	46
4	Cucugnan	Saint-Paul-de-Fenouillet	23.5 or 27.5km	1110 or 1330m	1150 or 1370m	7 or 9hr	54
5	Saint-Paul-de-Fenouillet	Caudiès-de-Fenouillèdes	22 or 13.5km	930 or 460m	840 or 370m	7 or 4hr	64
6	Caudiès-de-Fenouillèdes	Axat	21.75km	920m	850m	6hr	71
7	Axat	Quirbajou	12.25km	950m	550m	5hr	79
8	Quirbajou	Puivert	21.5km	600m	930m	6hr	84

Cucugnan to Puivert: north variant

4a	Cucugnan	Camps-sur-l'Agly	20.5 or 24.5km	1130 or 1350m	930 or 1150m	6½ or 8½hr	92
5a	Camps-sur-l'Agly	Bugarach	11.5km	580m	630m	4hr	96
6a	Bugarach	Quillan	23.25km	980m	1150m	7hr	101
7a	Quillan	Puivert	20km	840m	650m	6hr	108

Puivert to Foix

9	Puivert	Espezel	16.75km	650m	240m	5hr	111
10	Espezel	Comus	20km	730m	440m	6hr	117
11	Comus	Montségur	14km	700m	950m	5hr	123
12	Montségur	Roquefixade	16.5 or 17.75km	690m or 840m	840m or 990m	5 or 6½hr	129
13	Roquefixade	Foix	20.25 or 21km	680m or 745m	1060m or 1125m	6 or 7hr	134
Total (main route)			253km–267.5km	9990m–10,895m	9580m–10,485m	**13 days (75hr–82½hr)**	
Total (north variant)			235.75km–241.75km	9480m–9915m	9090m–9525m	**12 days (70½hr–75hr)**	

Walking toward Puilaurens Castle, its intact battlements stark against the sky (Stage 6)

INTRODUCTION

Quéribus Castle sitting above the Corbières landscape (Stage 3)

The Cathar Way, or *Sentier Cathare*, is a voyage into the past. A trail of some 260km through the foothills of the Pyrenees in Languedoc, southern France, it links a chain of ruined medieval castles and retraces the dark history of the Languedoc Cathars – a divergent Christian sect whose brutal fate would shift the very foundations of France.

The Cathars thrived in medieval Languedoc, then a fiercely independent region ruled by its own southern nobility. But this liberty was not to last: the Catholic Church declared the Cathars heretics and in 1209 launched a crusade against them in Languedoc. Meeting resistance from the outraged southerners, the crusaders soon wrought violent devastation on the whole region, and ultimately destroyed the autonomy of Languedoc forever.

The nine castles visited on the Cathar Way are known as the 'Cathar castles' and each has its own history, Cathar related and not. Most long since left to rack and ruin, these crumbling fortresses perched high on rocky pinnacles are still formidable sights to behold, and elicit the eerie feeling that this history is both long past, and yet almost within touching distance.

The trail also explores the wild, sun-baked Languedoc landscape. Beginning at the Mediterranean coast and ending far inland, it traverses the rocky hill ranges heading towards the Ariège Pyrenees, and meanders through woodland, vineyards, ancient villages, gorges and plateaux – including some places that have lain largely undisturbed for hundreds of years.

But beyond being simply a walking tour of Languedoc, the Cathar Way can tell us something of the human story of the Cathars: their lives, their deaths and the destruction of Languedoc as it was. We would echo the previous author of this guide in urging you to read more about the Cathars before you begin walking this trail, to fully appreciate the sites and what they represent – see Appendix E for some suggested titles.

LANGUEDOC HISTORY

The name 'Languedoc' comes from the phrase *langue d'Oc*, a reference to the Occitan language, then spoken all over the medieval provinces of what is now southern France. Languedoc at that time had little in common with the France of the north where, in contrast, the *langue d'Oïl* was spoken. It was a difference not just of languages and geography, but of whole kingdoms and cultures.

Medieval Languedoc was then a large, sprawling region, essentially free from the control of northern France, and broken up into disparate feudal principalities. These were governed by an extended assortment of lords, counts and barons, with the most powerful of all being the ruling Count of Toulouse.

Under this dissipated power structure, throughout the 12th century Languedoc grew and evolved. The region enjoyed a period of

The Boulzane River valley is one of many surprisingly remote sections on the Cathar Way (Stage 6)

increased trade and economic growth. The courts of the nobility had long been highly cultured places of entertainment and finery, attracting the famous roving troubadours – musical poets who sang about romantic love (notably in Occitan rather than Latin).

It was in this time and place of independence, increased prosperity and tolerance, with people and ideas freely intermingling along travel and trade routes, that Catharism began to take root and spread.

THE CATHARS AND THE CRUSADE

The Cathars were a Christian dualist sect that flourished in several parts of Western Europe in the Middle Ages, and in Languedoc particularly from the 12th century onwards. The name 'Cathars' was in fact coined by the Catholic medieval clerics who saw them as heretics, perhaps to imply a mocking 'pure' (the Latin *Cathari* derives from the Greek *katharoi* – 'the pure'). Along similar lines, the word for Cathar priests, 'Perfects', was actually shorthand for 'perfect heretic'. The names Cathars gave themselves were simply Christians and Good Men/Good Women (*Bons Hommes/ Bonnes Femmes*). Yet although they may have seen themselves as simple Christians, with growing popularity and beliefs markedly different from

the established church, the Cathars were in a dangerous position.

The radical Cathar belief that set them apart was the dualist idea that good and evil were separate governing principles. They concluded from this that physical (material) reality was in fact of evil creation, and that in order to gain salvation it had to be rejected. Perfects were therefore ascetic, eschewing wealth, marriage and social distinctions – women were also allowed into the ranks of the ordained. The Cathars gained followers throughout the classes, both rich and poor.

The Catholic establishment could not tolerate such a heretical diversion from the dogma of the Church. Several papal legates were sent to Languedoc in the latter part of the 12th century to preach and persuade, but to little avail. The lords of Languedoc, such as Raymond VI Count of Toulouse, didn't help much either; some of the nobility even had Cathar family members themselves.

Then in 1208 one of the legates, Pierre de Castelnau, was assassinated. It proved a turning point, as Pope Innocent III promptly pinned the blame on Raymond VI and called for a crusade against the Cathars.

And so began what would be known as the Albigensian Crusade, named after the nearby Languedoc town of Albi. The key events are summarised here, with castles on the Cathar Way highlighted in bold:

THE ALBIGENSIAN CRUSADE

1209 – Pope Innocent III launches a crusade against the Cathars of Languedoc and a host of soldiers is assembled from Northern France.

July 1209 – Sacking of the city of Béziers by French forces. In an act of astonishing violence, all inhabitants are slaughtered – Cathar and Catholic alike – and the city is razed.

August 1209 – Siege and quick surrender of the important city of Carcassonne. The young Viscount of Carcassonne and Béziers, Raymond Roger Trencavel, is imprisoned, but the people of Carcassonne are allowed to flee unharmed. Trencavel then dies in prison in November. A talented new military commander is appointed to lead the crusade: the ruthless Simon de Montfort (father of the better-known Simon de Montfort, 6th Earl of Leicester, considered one of the progenitors of modern parliamentary democracy).

Vertiginous sights from within Peyrepertuse Castle, on the windswept Saint-Louis stairs (Stage 4)

1210 – De Montfort attacks and successfully captures castles all over Languedoc, burning Cathars and killing anyone who resists. Termes Castle falls, as well as **Aguilar Castle** (Stage 2, abandoned by the Cathar family that owns Termes) and **Puivert Castle** (Stage 8). Infamously, at Bram the captured Cathars have their eyes gouged out and ears and lips cut off and are sent marching to nearby Lastours as a warning. Minerve settlement also surrenders and the Cathars living there choose to burn over recanting.

1211 – Cabaret (Lastours) surrenders, Lavaur falls, Toulouse is besieged, and the Battle of Castelnaudary erupts, where the Counts of Foix and Toulouse fail to defeat Simon de Montfort's superior forces.

1213 – Battle of Muret is fought and Peter II, the King of Aragon who had come to the aid of the south, is killed – a major blow to the south.

1215 – At the Fourth Lateran Council in Rome, Pope Innocent III reavows his condemnation of heresies such as the Cathars. Raymond VI of Toulouse is stripped of his titles and lands, which go to Simon de Montfort. **Foix Castle** (Stage 13) is also surrendered to the Pope's legate.

1217 – Raymond VI successfully takes back Toulouse.

1218 – Simon de Montfort is killed in a skirmish. Stories from the time suggest it was by a missile from a slingshot operated by women. His son Amaury succeeds him but steadily loses much of the lands his father held, and the crusade loses its impetus.

1226 – The crusade is relaunched by Louis VIII, the French king.

1229 – Treaty of Paris is signed and Raymond VII submits, annexing the Count of Toulouse's lands to France, signalling both the end of the crusade and effectively the end of Languedoc independence – but not the Cathar influence.

1233 – Pope Gregory IX launches the Inquisition in Languedoc to root out the remaining Cathars. The pitiless Inquisitors become a much-hated presence in the region.

1240 – A band of knights led by Raymond de Trencavel attempts and fails to take back Carcassonne. **Peyrepertuse Castle** (Stage 4) falls.

1242 – Inquisition officials are murdered in Avignonet by Cathar knights from Montségur.

1243–1244 – **Montségur Castle** (Stage 11) is besieged over a long and bitter winter. Eventually surrendering, the Cathars who sheltered there are ordered to repent or die and 225 Cathars perish in a mass burning at the castle base.

1255 – Surrender of **Quéribus Castle** (Stage 3), one of the last redoubts of the Cathars, after the capture of Cathar lord Chabert de Barbaira. At a similar time, the king of France orders fortifications to be added to **Puilaurens Castle**

(Stage 6), also previously connected to Barbaira, signifying control of this castle as well.

1258 – Treaty of Corbeil is signed between Louis IX of France and James I of Aragon to establish the frontier between France and Aragon. Many of the former Cathar castles are repurposed to defend the new border.

1317 – The Inquisition in the village of Montaillou creates a startlingly detailed record of medieval rural life, later used by historian Emmanuel Le Roy Ladurie in his book *Montaillou*.

1321 – Last-known Languedoc Perfect Guilhem Bélibaste – a Cathar who was originally from Cubières-sur-Cinoble (Stage 4a) – is burned at the stake in Villerouge-Termenès.

1659 – Treaty of the Pyrenees is signed between France and Spain, moving the border between the two countries further south, rendering the former Cathar castles obsolete as border defences. Most are abandoned to the elements.

THE CATHAR WAY ROUTE

Originally, the Cathar Way was a composite route, made up of other long-distance paths strung together to allow visitors to approach the Cathar castles on foot, but now it is officially a *Grande Randonnée* path – the GR367. Beginning in the coastal town of Port-la-Nouvelle and ending in the medieval city of Foix, it comprises 260km of ancient footpaths, jeep tracks and country lanes, sweeping from sea level to 1300m altitude across the rugged hill ranges of the Corbières and the Fenouillèdes.

The Cathar Way splits in Stage 4, offering two main options: the main route as described here trips along to the south – becoming the GR367A for the duration of the split – and links up all nine Cathar castles; while a variant heads off to the north, keeping the GR367 markings, an option

First view of Montségur Castle from the Plateau de Languerail (Stage 10)

that misses some Cathar castles to make a more direct and still beautiful walk. The options rejoin at Coudons (Stage 8) and are further discussed below.

There is also a smaller diversion of note, on Stage 5: an ancient track that runs from Prugnanes to the stage end at Caudiès-de-Fenouillèdes, accompanied by faded waymarks. It's quicker and lower in elevation than the official route. As this is no longer the official Cathar Way it isn't expounded on here, but directions to it are provided when it intersects with the official Cathar Way as it is now.

The level of difficulty on the Cathar Way differs from day to day. Some stages are gentle walks through rolling hills, while others can feel quite strenuous, heading up steep, rocky paths with as much as 1000m of elevation in a day. Remember also that a lot of the route is in open countryside with little shade, and in southern France the temperature and sun strength will drastically affect how difficult you find these days.

FEATURES OF INTEREST

Cathar castles on the Cathar Way

The Cathar Way takes in nine of the so-called 'Cathar castles' – medieval fortifications built on impossibly high and jagged rocky precipices. Most of these structures are now ruins and, having been employed for a range of uses over the years, don't really resemble what they would've looked like in the early 13th century. But most do have roots in Cathar history, and so the sheer daring of their location and construction tells us much of the might and influence of Languedoc as it was.

All are open to the public and most charge admission of a few euros apiece. Some have small shops where visitors can buy books and souvenirs. Although generally open throughout the year, some close for a month or two in winter, and at short notice in high winds.

The Cathar castles on the Cathar Way are:

- Aguilar (Stage 2)
- Quéribus (Stage 3)
- Peyrepertuse (Stage 4)
- Fenouillet (Stage 6)
- Puilaurens (Stage 6)
- Puivert (Stage 8)
- Montségur (Stage 11)
- Roquefixade (Stage 12)
- Foix (Stage 13)

Other features

As well as Cathar history, the trail does have plenty of other interesting features. The mountains, caves and forests of Cathar country are mysterious places, riddled with stories and legends about hidden treasure, the Knights Templar, and even the Holy Grail.

Many of the villages you will walk through are over 1000 years old, each with its own agrarian history.

Winemaking is a proud tradition, with towns like Tuchan and Cucugnan surrounded by vineyards. The harvest in October is a particularly busy time of year, when truckloads of grapes can be seen trundling around the narrow streets.

This area was a key agitation point of the French Resistance in World War II. You'll pass memorials to Resistance fighters, like the one just outside Roquefixade (Stage 12) or the reconstructed French Resistance HQ hut on Stage 9.

PLANNING THE WALK

The Cathar Way can be walked in either direction, but here it is described from east to west, ending with a run of three stupendous Cathar castles: Montségur, Roquefixade and Foix.

This guide breaks up the route into 13 day-stages, with the north variant providing four alternative stages that split off in Stage 4 and run parallel around the middle of the route.

The Cathar Way is a well-known but remarkably remote walk; there may be days where you don't see anyone and don't really pass through much in the way of inhabited settlements. There may be no shops for a day or more, particularly on the second half of the route, so it's important to check this guide so that you can know what's ahead and stock up accordingly – see the amenities list in Appendix A.

NORTH VARIANT

The north variant, stretching 46.5km, breaks away from the main route in Stage 4 and then rejoins it in Stage 8. It is around 26km shorter than the parallel section of the main route, making the overall length of the trail doing this variation 236km. When choosing which option to go for, take into consideration that the north variant omits the castles of Fenouillet and Puilaurens (both on Stage 6) and does not include any others. However, it does take in the pretty (and useful) town of Quillan (Stage 6a), the imposing mountain ridge of the Pech de Bugarach, and some interesting historical sites relating to the French Resistance in World War II.

Both options are at times isolated, but the north variant perhaps goes deeper into the more remote parts of Languedoc. Note also that the north variant is walked over four stages in comparison to the south (main) route's five, so the final northern Stage 7a braids back in with Stage 8 on the main route, rejoining it for good at Stage 9.

ALTERNATIVE WAYS TO STAGE THE CATHAR WAY

There are multiple ways to stage the Cathar Way, depending on your purpose and speed. As well as the 13-day schedule described in detail in this guide, there are the following possibilities:

The Cathar Way in 12 days

All stages as in this guide except 5–7 which are merged into two days as follows:

- Day 5 Saint-Paul to Puilaurens (33.25km, or 24.5km via ancient route)
- Day 6 Puilaurens to Quirbajou (22.5km)

Quickest way of seeing all the castles

- Day 1 Tuchan to Duilhac (22.25km)
- Day 2 Duilhac to Prugnanes (26km using ancient route)
- Day 3 Prugnanes to Puilaurens (17.5km)
- Day 4 Puilaurens to Quirbajou (22.5km)
- Day 5 Quirbajou to Puivert (21.5km)
- Day 6 Puivert to Espezel (16.75km)
- Day 7 Espezel to Comus (20km)
- Day 8 Comus to Montferrier (19.5km)
- Day 9 Montferrier to Foix (31km)

Mixing the main route and the north variant

- Stage 1–3 as in this guide
- Day 4 Cucugnan to Camps-sur-l'Agly (20.5km)
- Day 5 Camps-sur-l'Agly to Puilaurens (24.25km)
- Day 6 Puilaurens to Quirbajou (22.5km)
- Day 7 Quirbajou to Puivert (21.5km)

- Day 8 Puivert to Comus (36.5km)
- Day 9 Comus to Montferrier (19.5km)
- Day 10 Montferrier to Foix (31km)

GETTING THERE

Getting to Cathar country from the UK entirely by train is very possible. Take the Eurostar from London St Pancras to Paris or Lille, then change onto France's famous high-speed TGV (*trains à grande vitesse*) to reach Toulouse, Narbonne or Perpignan. From there take a regional train to Port-la-Nouvelle, the start of the walk.

If arriving from European countries north and east of the route by rail, head to Narbonne for a regional connection to the trailhead at Port-la-Nouvelle. If travelling from Spain by rail, connect in Perpignan for the same regional service.

If flying from the UK, Béziers is the most convenient place to arrive into – as well as being the most relevant to Cathar history. Its airport is served by Ryanair from London Luton, Bristol, Edinburgh and Manchester.

To get to the start of the walk from Béziers airport, take the bus (20min) into the city and then the train out to Narbonne, and change trains to get to Port-la-Nouvelle, where the walk starts directly out of the train station. However, we recommend staying a day or two in Béziers, which is the site of one of the earliest and most infamous aggressions of the Albigensian

Bridge over the Rébenty River in Marsa (Stage 7)

Crusade and has some fascinating ancient sites as well as plentiful resources on Cathar history.

Alternatively, you can fly into Toulouse, Carcassonne or Perpignan, which each have scheduled flights from all over Britain and Ireland offered by Ryanair, Flybe, Jet2 and British Airways.

In order to reach the area from other parts of the world it may be worth travelling via London; or the main relevant airports are Paris, Nice, Lyon, Toulouse and Marseille. All of these have rail and bus connections to Cathar country – namely to Toulouse or Perpignan.

From Toulouse and Carcassonne airports you can also take the train to Narbonne and then onto Port-la-Nouvelle. From Perpignan you again take a regional train directly to Port-la-Nouvelle.

Long-distance coach travel to Cathar country is possible, with companies such as Omio and FlixBus running routes to Perpignan and Toulouse from across Europe. But for comfort, convenience and comparable cost, rail networks are preferable.

At the end of the walk at Foix, the train station has a direct line to Toulouse.

GETTING AROUND

Although it's easy to get to Languedoc, moving between locations on the walk is tricker as public transport is very limited.

Port-la-Nouvelle and Foix are both connected to the rail network, but virtually none of the other locations on the walk are. The only available option is the Train du Pays Cathare et du Fenouillèdes (also known as *Le*

Train Rouge, the Red Train) – a tourist train running in the summer between Rivesaltes and Axat (Stage 7), via St-Paul-de-Fenouillet (Stage 5) and Caudiès-de-Fenouillèdes (Stage 6). See Appendix C for details.

Buses that do exist function mainly for locals and school runs. There are, however, two useful bus routes: between Carcassonne and Quillan (Stage 7a) – a rail replacement bus as the Quillan railway station is no longer in use – and another between Perpignan and Quillan. Running a few times a day but at potentially inconvenient times, these buses are at least very cheap, with fares at just €2 in 2021. See the beginning of each stage description for specific information, and again, Appendix C for further information on timetables and tickets.

There are taxis in the region, but they are also generally limited and extraordinarily expensive. Appendix C has some suggested services, or you could ask hoteliers for local recommendations.

WHEN TO GO

The best time of year to walk the Cathar Way is either between April and June or between September and October. Walking in the high summer months can be much more difficult due to the heat, plus accommodation is busier with holidaymakers and more expensive. In the winter months accommodation may be closed, and with the route ascending to over

1300m some of the highest areas may be impacted by snow.

ACCOMMODATION

Planning your accommodation for the Cathar Way does require a bit of effort as not every town/village on the trail has facilities. However, the area offers something to suit most budgets, with everything from camping to luxury. See Appendix B for a select list of options for each of the stages, including our own recommendations.

The types of accommodation you can expect to find are as follows.

Most commonly found on the trail are *chambres d'hôtes* – guest houses or B&Bs that vary in style but are usually very comfortable. Most include breakfast and some even offer evening meals (*table d'hôte*) as an extra.

Gîtes d'étape are also popular – an unfussy accommodation style similar to a youth hostel and ideal for walkers and cyclists. They sometimes offer meals as well.

Alternatively there is the odd *auberge* – an inn that traditionally has a restaurant attached to it, common to rural parts of France.

And of course there's also a range of hotels, mostly found in the cities and towns. Logis is a modestly priced, common and reliable brand in the local area.

Camping is an ever-popular pastime in France and campsites with facilities are peppered over the course of the Cathar Way – although there are enough budget accommodation options to mean this is not a necessity. Camping the entire route would only be possible with at least some wild camping, which isn't an accepted practice in France on private land without permission from the landowner. This can be sought and given, but if it's not, you run the risk of local ire.

While the Cathar Way is not an overwhelmingly busy walk, this area is a popular tourist destination, particularly in summer. As some of the accommodation is very limited in capacity, booking in advance is a good idea – something that can be done easily online for most places.

FOOD AND DRINK

The Cathar Way is characterised by its peace and remoteness, so the opportunities to pick up food and refreshments are sporadic. The stages do generally end in small villages or towns, but not all of these places have useful shops or cafés, so it's important to know what's ahead of you and to prepare. See Appendix A for a list of places along the Cathar Way that have amenities like shops, restaurants and ATM machines (the last of these being a particular rarity).

There are at least a fair amount of drinking-water taps in many of the sleepy little places you'll walk through – these are pointed out in the route notes and maps.

The local cuisine revolves around produce grown, reared or hunted on the local hillsides and valleys. Wild boar meat, cured pork sausage and goat's cheese are all enthusiastically offered, as well as seasonal earthy vegetables – paired of course with the excellent Languedoc wine.

LANGUAGE

French is spoken in Languedoc, but also Occitan more locally. You may see some town signs that are in French on one side and Occitan on the other.

Corbières at the beginning of the trail is famous for its viticulture

Many locals do speak some English, but not all – particularly in the small rural villages you'll be walking through. Having some knowledge of basic French will help considerably; see Appendix D for some words and phrases relevant to the trail.

MONEY MATTERS

France uses the euro (€), and places in the cities and big towns on the Cathar Way would have no problem taking Visa or MasterCard.

The very small shops and cafés, and some types of basic accommodation, may not always take card however, so it's important to carry cash with you.

There are some ATMs along the route but they are not particularly frequent and not necessarily where you'd hope them to be. Consult Appendix A for a list of places with bank machines.

Languedoc is not an especially expensive region of France – in fact it compares very favourably to its neighbour Provence. Cafés and groceries are inexpensive and, being a wine region, there are some great local wine deals, especially in restaurants.

PHONE AND WI-FI

The French dialling code is 33. Mobile phone reception is surprisingly good on the Cathar Way itself; there's 3G signal in places, and 4G is common in the towns and cities. Wi-Fi is widely available in the *gîtes* and hotels.

HEALTH AND SAFETY

Although this is a generally gentle and safe walk on well-made paths, there are a few things to be aware of, and it always makes good sense to have the emergency numbers to hand.

EMERGENCY NUMBERS

- General European emergency number: 112
- *Sapeurs-pompiers* (fire service, which can deal with accidents and injuries): 18
- Medical emergency: 15
- Police: 17

As hiking is technically classed as a sport, you should make sure your travel insurance adequately covers your trip.

You'll find pharmacies in villages along the route; these should be your first port of call for medical services. They can recommend and direct you to local doctors or surgeries if you need them. Hospitals are in Perpignan, Narbonne, Carcassonne and Béziers.

Some of the terrain on the Cathar Way can be loose and rocky. Pay attention to your footing, particularly on steep descents.

Possibly the most pressing concern on this trail is **dehydration**; in a hot and dry climate like this it's easy to underestimate how much water you will need to carry. Using a water bladder is a good way to stay hydrated, as well as remembering to stop and refill at the taps in the villages. **Sun exposure** could be a problem as long sections of this trail offer little shade. As summer temperatures can reach over 40°C it's important that as well as staying hydrated you wear a hat and sunscreen, and make sure to take regular breaks in the shade where possible. There have been instances of forest fires in some of the driest areas in midsummer – a time of year we wouldn't recommend walking this trail.

Big **electric storms** can brew and burst in Languedoc, particularly in the summer. Doing most of your walking in the first part of the day can reduce the risk of getting caught in a storm, as they tend to build in the afternoon. But if you are caught in one it's best to get indoors if possible, and avoid sheltering under lone trees.

Wild animals aren't something to be overly worried about, but the area does have its share. The extensive woodland is home to wild boar – a timid species which you nevertheless wouldn't want to startle or separate from their young. Bears, although recorded as straying into these foothills from time to time, are not resident and your chance of seeing one is once-in-a-lifetime small. There are a few species of **snake** in Languedoc, although most aren't venomous or commonly seen. Stay on the path and away from long grass to avoid them. In the highly unlikely event that you are bitten, keep the wound lower than the heart, wash it and cover it with

a clean, dry dressing. Seek medical advice as soon as possible.

Languedoc has become a breeding ground for **processionary caterpillars** – a non-native species that can be seen on the lusher parts of the trail wreaking their hungry havoc on local vegetation. They suspend themselves on thin thread before forming long lines along the forest floor. They can cause a nasty or even severe stinging reaction if touched, and can be deadly to dogs, so steer well clear. If you are stung, remove the sting and clean the area around it. If swelling persists, or it causes more serious allergic responses – like vomiting, or an asthma attack – seek prompt medical help.

Hunting, mostly for boar, is a popular pastime in Languedoc and parts of the trail go through hunting areas – you may see signs ('*chasse gardée*') alerting walkers to hunters nearby. It's fine to continue but good sense to always stay on the path – and it doesn't hurt to be wearing an item of bright clothing.

Dogs are commonly used in farming and hunting in Languedoc. The most notable is the Pyrenean mountain dog – a large shaggy animal reared to guard sheep. If you see one, give it and its flock a wide berth and there shouldn't be a problem. Do not approach these dogs, go around them (off-route if necessary) or wait for them to leave. It's not really recommended to bring your own dog on a long-distance trail, but if you do, make sure to keep it away from livestock and other dogs.

WHAT TO TAKE

Hiking kit requirements only really vary with changes of season, so below is a (not exhaustive) list of useful items assuming the warm weather that tends to prevail in Languedoc. It's worth nothing, though, that even in summer on the high points of the trail it can be cold, hence the inclusion of warm layers. The list doesn't include camping gear as although it's possible to camp on the Cathar Way there are plenty of budget accommodation options available.

Packing list
- Walking rucksack (at least 35L, limiting the weight to around 10kg)
- Sturdy walking boots
- Sandals
- Waterproof jacket and (if preferred) trousers
- Two layers of fast-drying outdoor clothing
- Hats for both shade and warmth
- Gloves
- Down jacket
- Guidebook and map
- Water bladder (2L capacity)
- Poles (not required but recommended)
- Mobile phone and charger
- Camera and charger
- Cash and cards
- Plug adapter
- Hand sanitiser
- First aid kit
- Sunscreen
- Energy bars (bringing a bulk from home will be cheaper)
- GPS tracker (if using)

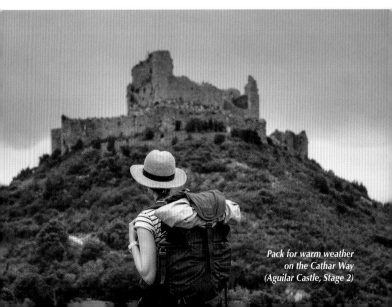

Pack for warm weather on the Cathar Way (Aguilar Castle, Stage 2)

MAPS

The maps in this book should be helpful but a full-sized map is invaluable. The most useful is the 1:50,000 *Le Sentier Cathare* map published by Rando Éditions. It covers the whole trail and other local walking routes, and orientates you to the wider area (it makes a good souvenir too). You can buy it online before you leave home, but shops along the trail also sell it.

There are also 1:25,000 maps by IGN which are much more detailed, but the route has changed a bit since they were published, and it's not really practical to carry all eight of them on the route anyway.

The AllTrails mapping app gives useful information on the geography of the route and surrounding area.

WAYMARKING

As the Cathar Way has official GR status, you will be wholly following red-and-white striped *balises* (waymarks), although you may at times still see the old blue-and-yellow ones as well. The two parallel lines are often painted on trees or rocks, while two stripes making a cross indicate that the path ahead is the wrong way. The trail is generally very well waymarked, with several 'Cathar Way' ('*Sentier Cathare*') signposts having also been erected. The main route is simply signposted as the 'Sentier Cathare', sometimes with 'GR367A'; while the northern variant is 'Sentier Cathare Nord', also sometimes with 'GR367'.

Within the crumbling walls of Aguilar Castle, looking out onto the Cathar Way (Stage 2)

Other long-distance paths

The Cathar Way joins and crosses several other long-distance trails which you will also see signposted. These are summarised below.

Between Peyrepertuse in Stage 4 and Caudiès-de-Fenouillèdes in Stage 5 the route weaves at times with the GR36, a path running the length of France from Normandy to the Pyrenees mountains.

Between Coudons and Puivert in Stage 8 the route buddies up with the GR7, also known as the E4 – a European long-distance path that starts in Tarifa, Spain and ends in the Peloponnese, Greece.

When you rejoin the GR7(B) at Comus and follow it until Montségur

Peyrepertuse Castle (built into the cliff) looks onto the route (Stage 4)

on Stage 10, you are also following a third trail: the G107, which the Cathar Way then runs alongside for all of Stages 11, 12 and 13. Called Le Chemin des Bonshommes (The Goodmen's Trail), it was created to retrace the journey Cathars took to cross the Pyrenees, and connects Foix with Andorra and Spain.

UPDATES

There have been four major updates to this guide since the previous edition. First is the sizeable detour to the town of Saint-Paul-de-Fenouillet in Stage 4; secondly a new section diverts up over Roc Paradet to the isolated Campeau plateau in Stage 5;

and third is the modified final stretch into the city of Foix at the end of Stage 13. These changes have lengthened the route as it was; therefore, fourthly, this new edition is one stage longer than previous guides.

While these changes are to all intents and purposes permanent and so included, you may well encounter temporary diversions that aren't mentioned here – for instance in tree-felling areas. Pay close attention to the waymarks in the local area, which will still be clearly marked.

USING THIS GUIDE

The route is broken up in this guide into 13 day-stages, with all the key information on each stage compiled into the route summary table at the beginning of the book. This includes the essential statistics: distance, time, ascent and descent.

Within the route description, the following information is provided for each stage.

Key information: Each stage opens with a box showing key data for the stage (start, finish, distance, ascent, descent and time), along with details of possible transport links and places to stop for food and drink en route.

Stage summary: This gives a brief overview of the route ahead, its level of difficulty and type(s) of terrain.

Map: The stage routes are mapped on 1:100,000 maps derived from open-source data, which although accurate should not replace the use of a more detailed map. (See 'Maps', above.)

Route notes: A detailed description of the day's walk then follows. Places and landmarks shown in **bold** correlate with the stage map, for orientation.

Points of interest: These provide brief background information about the landmarks and other sites of interest encountered on the Cathar Way.

Also included are notes on possible food and drink stops along the route and a bit of information about the end-place of each stage, which is usually a village or small town.

GPX tracks

GPX tracks for the routes in this guide-book are available to download free at www.cicerone.co.uk/1047/GPX. If you have not bought the book through the Cicerone website, or have bought the book without opening an account, please register your purchase in your Cicerone library to access GPX and update information.

A GPS device is an excellent aid to navigation, but you should also carry a map and compass and know how to use them. GPX files are provided in good faith, but in view of the profusion of formats and devices, neither the authors nor the publisher accept responsibility for their use. We provide files in a single standard GPX format that works on most devices and systems, but you may need to convert files to your preferred format using a GPX converter such as gpsvisualizer.com or one of the many other apps and online converters available.

THE CATHAR WAY

Puilaurens Castle from the trail (Stage 6)

PORT-LA-NOUVELLE TO PUIVERT

STAGE 1
Port-la-Nouvelle to Durban-Corbières

Start	Port-la-Nouvelle rail station
Finish	Durban-Corbières town centre
Distance	27.5km
Ascent	710m
Descent	620m
Time	7hr
Refreshments	Port-la-Nouvelle has a supermarket along with a campsite to fill up on water. There are also some small restaurants on the outskirts of the village of Roquefort-des-Corbières and Durban-Corbières has most amenities including a food shop.
Public transport	There are direct trains between Port-la-Nouvelle and Perpignan. Train connections are from Béziers, or from Carcassonne and Toulouse via Narbonne.

Stage 1 of the Cathar Way is distinct from the other stages: rather than involving castles and mountain villages, the route starts near the sea and heads into Mediterranean coastal countryside, traversing rugged *garrigue* (a type of scrubland), wide-open limestone plateaux and tranquil Corbières vineyards. Think of this stage as being less about the Cathars and more about quiet and strikingly wild landscapes.

It is quite a long day, with plenty of ascent, so there is an option to divide it into two by stopping after 19km at the D205 road. The only accommodation is a rural B&B – Domaine Castelsec – which is just under 2km away to the north and does evening meals. Contact the owner to check if it's possible to be picked up and dropped off the next morning to continue the journey.

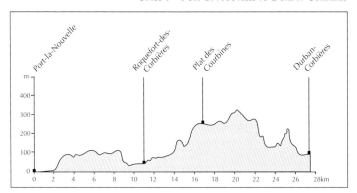

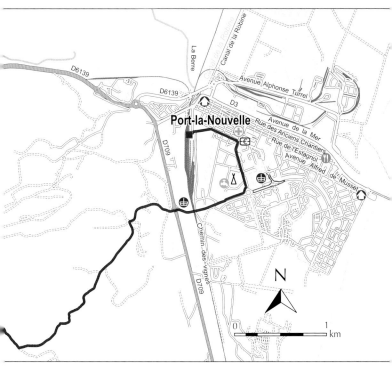

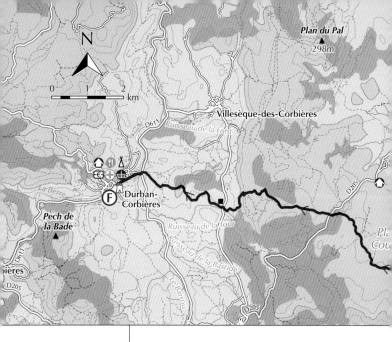

To begin the Cathar Way, exit the railway station in **Port-la-Nouvelle** and turn left through the car park onto Avenue Jean Moulin. Turn right and follow it towards the coast.

> **Port-la-Nouvelle** is an unassuming coastal town which does boast long sections of wide sandy beach. If you've arrived here having walked the Cathar Way from west to east, you might well be tempted to dip your toes in the sea.

At the road end turn right onto Boulevard l'Avenir and walk to a roundabout. Take the right turning down the road lined with palm trees that bends to the left. Pass a sports centre, then a **campsite** on your right, and just before another roundabout take the footpath on the right, marked with a yellow Cathar Way sign. This gives a brief respite from the road, so follow it for 250 metres before crossing back over the road as marked

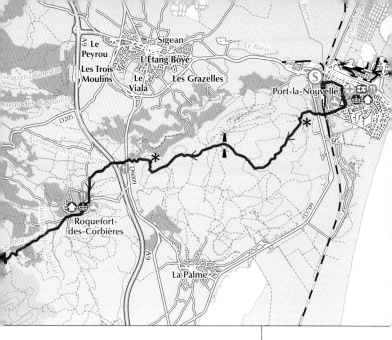

by the red-and-white *balise* (waymark). Continue over the bridge to reach another roundabout with an ALDI **supermarket** off to the right. From here take the gravel track leading up into the hills as waymarked.

> There is also a **small scallop shell waymark** here, the symbol of the pilgrimage route Voie de Piémont. It starts in Narbonne and heads to Santiago de Compostela in Spain, slicing through the Pyrenees as it goes.

After 200 metres on the gravel track continue uphill to the left, signposted Cathar Way GR367. Shortly afterwards pass a local footpath map on the right, ignoring the track on the left. After a further 400 metres there are two parking areas – one on either side of the path. ▶

Carry straight on between the car parks to reach a three-way fork of tracks shortly afterwards. Take the furthest left. A little further on the path forks again: go to

From the viewing platform in the car park on the left there are expansive views of industrial Port-la-Nouvelle and the vast ocean beyond.

the right to walk over a wide open limestone plateau, sparsely vegetated save for a few wild herbs. After just over 1km follow the rocky path as it bends slightly to the right and descends into a small valley. Walk through the valley for another 1km to reach a T-junction with a '*Garrigue Haute*' signpost (meaning an area of high coastal scrubland).

FLORA

There's a beautiful and aromatic array of flowers and plants on this coastal part of the Cathar Way, particularly of course in spring. The most commonly found in this area are wild thyme, rosemary and the bright pink *Cistus albidus* (grey-leaved cistus).

On later sections of the route these are joined by a riot of other flora, including those particular to the Pyrenees like the beautiful *Fritillaria nigra* (Pyrenean fritillary) and the *Lilium pyrenaicum* (Pyrenean lily).

Turn right towards the wind turbines – a dominant feature in the bare landscape here. After 800 metres there is a drive and a short avenue of cypress trees that leads to a farmhouse. Turn right, away from the house, and continue towards the turbines. Take the dirt track to the left at the fork 100 metres further on.

Walking over the rocky garrigue and away from the Mediterranean Sea

Go straight ahead when you reach a crossroads of tracks between the **wind turbines**. After a further 200 metres the path forks, with both ways signposted for

the Cathar Way. Take the left, going downhill towards Roquefort-des-Corbières. Pass a ruined building on the right, and then at another fork continue to the right, as signposted, for 1km.

When you near a wind turbine and a track joins from the left, continue straight on. After 400 metres take another track to the right, following it across scrubland to emerge at a wide **view** of the Mediterranean Sea and an inland lagoon.

A couple of hundred metres further on there is another fork. Take the footpath to the left towards the precipitous edge of the limestone cliff. Descend the steep rocky path (it's rather loose in parts); you'll see the beginnings of the famous Corbières vineyards below. When you reach the first vineyard continue straight on the path through the undergrowth to emerge at more vines, joining an established winemakers' track and following it to the left.

This track skirts the edges of more vine plots and soon becomes a tarmac lane. The lane quickly comes to another road, which you follow through a little tunnel under the D6009 road. ▶

If you're in need of refreshments there are a couple of places up on the D6009 to the left, the nearest being only 250 metres away.

Out of the tunnel, follow the road to the right and pass under the **A9 motorway**. Beyond the bridge, Roquefort-des-Corbières comes into view. Follow this road, with vineyards on the left, and after 800 metres take the left turn towards the village. As the lane draws closer to Roquefort, the limestone escarpment behind the village looms larger and ever more dramatic.

On entering **Roquefort-des-Corbières** go straight across at the crossroads and up Rue du Rocher de Cancale, passing a lovely little mural of the village on the right. ▶ After 80 metres turn right into Rue Los Castanhers and go across two more crossroads, passing the *mairie* (town hall) and a small selection of shops to reach a T-junction. Turn left up Rue des Trois Moulins.

Just up this street there is a drinking tap in the wall.

At the top of the street turn right and then right again onto Rue du Camin del Bosc. Follow this level road for 200 metres to reach a fork. Take the road to the right, which soon becomes Chemin de la Trillole, rising out of the village back into the countryside.

From this road there are eye-catching views across vineyards to **Pic du Pied du Poul** (596m). This is the eastern end of the Corbières Massif (also known as the Corbières Maritimes), an impressive set of Pyrenean foothills.

At the next fork keep left on the principal lane, and after another 500 metres take a right turn. Follow this lane for 1km until the tarmac ends at a fork, and then continue on the more established track to the left uphill.

Climb steadily on the track for 750 metres to reach a T-junction. Turn right here and snake downwards into a pretty vineyard valley shaped like an amphitheatre. Before reaching the bottom, on a left-hand bend, take a footpath off to the right.

Continue downhill on a rocky path, steep at times, but only for 200 metres or so. Follow the path sharply to the left and begin another climb, again steep in places.

Ignore a path off to the left after 500 metres and continue uphill. ◀ The path soon levels out and you begin to cross the second limestone plateau of the stage – the expansive **Plat des Courbines**. After 750 metres walking on a level path, at a fork, ignore the grassy track to the left and continue to the right. At another fork 100 metres later go left.

Follow this path, ignoring any small side-tracks, for nearly 2km. After entering a conifer plantation you'll reach a three-way fork: take the small footpath in the middle. This rocky little path goes deeper into the conifers and weaves its way out of the trees to the **D205 road**. ◀

To continue on the route, cross the road and walk uphill beyond the barrier on the concrete track, which soon turns to gravel. At a fork ignore a smaller track off to the left and continue descending for 300 metres through fragrant bushes of wild rosemary and thyme until you reach a left turning which is signposted.

Turn left here and almost immediately turn left again onto a footpath through undergrowth. Come out onto the track and turn left. Soon after at a grassy fork,

You may see signs to the Bornes Milliaires. These are two Roman milestones from the Augustan era, intended to guide travellers and pay homage to the emperor

This is where you can split the day if preferred, and stay at the B&B 2km along this road to the right.

ignore the track to the left and keep on the waymarked route to the right.

With a field on the left and a circular stone ruin on the right, skirt around the perimeter of the field. The path then becomes rocky, climbs a little and bears left. Where it bears left, turn right on a smaller waymarked path and soon come to the edge of a limestone cliff with a patchwork of vineyards, fields and farmsteads below, including a red-roofed **barn**.

Take care going downhill on the rocky path, which zigzags sharply at first and then becomes easier as it follows the contours of the hill. When you reach the field on the valley floor, skirt round its edge to meet the road opposite the red-roofed barn. Cross the road and walk along the track to the left of it.

Follow this flat track for 500 metres and then take the main track uphill away from a vineyard. The track soon bends round to the left and then to the right where it takes you through a small clearing with more vineyards visible beyond.

Follow this vineyard path into a little valley. Follow it to the edge of the vines at the corner of the plot, where the path continues into a thicket of small pine and other Mediterranean vegetation. Ascend gradually for 500 metres to reach a sort of fork, taking the steep (at first) footpath up to the left. The ascent only lasts for 200 metres, at which point you see your goal of Durban-Corbières, sitting in a new valley.

After the Plat des Courbines you descend to more vineyard-clad valleys

37

The descent that follows is steep in places and rocky throughout, but you soon come to an easier gravel track which follows an old stone wall. Emerge in due course at a vineyard on the left and a small cottage on the right. After the cottage the track becomes concrete and descends to meet a small tarmac lane. Continue straight on for a short way before turning left onto the larger D611. Cross over the river bridge and follow the road into **Durban-Corbières**.

DURBAN-CORBIÈRES

This ancient town sits peacefully on the banks of the River Berre and has the eye-catching ruins of a castle hunched over its streets. Really a manor house of sorts, all that remains of the castle, which dates to the 11th century, are intact 16th-century windows, and it doesn't appear to have either much connection to the Cathars or a defensive use. The ruins aren't open to the public but they are an arresting sight nonetheless.

Durban-Corbières Castle

Durban-Corbières is a useful town for walkers, with a fair few *chambres d'hôtes* to choose from as well as a café and restaurant. The local library has some tourist information leaflets in English and the shop sells a range of guidebooks and maps along with the usual array of foodstuffs.

STAGE 2
Durban-Corbières to Tuchan

Start	Durban-Corbières town centre
Finish	Tuchan town centre
Distance	27.5km
Ascent	1000m
Descent	930m
Time	8hr (or 8½hr including visit to Aguilar Castle)
Refreshments	Durban-Corbières has a useful grocery shop and a couple of restaurant/cafés, then nothing until Tuchan
Public transport	Bus 408 from Narbonne serves Durban-Corbières

Hot off the heels of a long first day, the second stage is another lengthy undertaking. It crosses three separate hill ridges, ascending and descending each. Combined with the length and the previous day's efforts, it is quite a challenging section.

The landscape does slowly change over the longer course of the stage: the vineyards and *garrigue* still dominate, but the route also takes you along rivers and down into forests. You will also get to your first Cathar castle: the impressive Aguilar Castle, near the end of the day's route.

Overall though, Stage 2 has a remote, uninhabited air. The one village passed – Embres-et-Castelmaure – has little in it so make sure you take water and supplies for the entire way.

From the bank of the River Berre in **Durban-Corbières**, walk along the main road with the river on the right. After 600 metres take the waymarked left up a little lane, leaving the town.

Snake uphill on a gravel track, rising above vineyards on the left and ignoring any side turnings. At a fork stay on the main track to the right. The path levels out to skirt the side of the hill. At another fork keep to the right and you'll see a waymark on the tree just ahead.

Soon you come to a three-way meeting of tracks: simply take the waymarked path downhill to the right. At

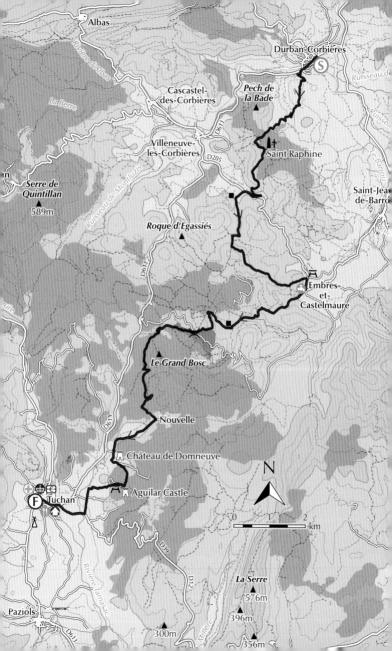

Albas

Rivière d'Albas

la Berre

Durban-Corbières

(S)

Ruisseau d

*Pech de
la Bade*

Cascastel-
des-Corbières

D611

le Barrou

Villeneuve-
les-Corbières

D205

Saint Raphine

Saint-Jea
de-Barro

*Serre de
Quintillan*
▲
589m

Ruisseau de Montfuzic

Roque d'Egassiés ▲

D611

Embres-
et-
Castelmaure

Le Grand Bosc ▲

D611

Nouvelle

Château de Domneuve

Aguilar Castle

(F) Tuchan

N

0   1   2
km

D39

D12

La Serre

576m
▲

396m
▲

300m
▲

356m
▲

Paziols

D611

Rivière Tamaricx

Rivière Tamaricx

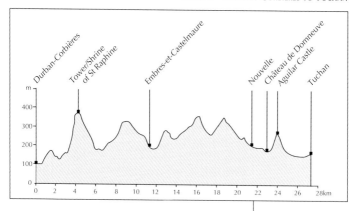

the bottom of this descent the track narrows with dense vegetation either side. Come out into a little valley on a wider gravel track and follow it to the valley bottom and a stream.

Swing right and cross the stream over a concrete bridge, soon afterwards turning left uphill on a concrete track. After 200 metres turn left and follow an earth track between vineyards for a short way. Take the first right to follow the perimeter of the vineyard. Ignore a side turning and stay on the dirt track as it ascends. At the top of this short climb, keep right, and after another climb come to a T-junction: take the footpath to the right into woodland.

Walk through the woods for 100 metres to reach a fork and take the right turn uphill. This is the first of the big hills of this stage and it is quite an arduous climb on a footpath roughed up with roots and rocks, which could be made more difficult if there has been heavy rain.

At a crossroads continue straight ahead uphill. Soon after, you emerge at the top – which can be windy – and the **tall tower and shrine of Saint Raphine**, which you might have spotted from the valley. ▶ From the shrine continue downhill on the clear, wide track. Descend easily for 1.5km and turn left at a T-junction. At the valley bottom turn sharply back on yourself to the right, the path rising slightly to meet the **D205**.

There are two beautiful views here: looking back at Durban-Corbières and then onwards to the next valley.

41

If you want to **shorten** this long and arduous day slightly, there's the option of turning left here and following the D205 directly into Embres-et-Castelmaure, rather than taking the more scenic walking route. This would save about 1.5km and 100m of ascent and descent.

Turn right onto the D205 and walk for 400 metres before taking a gravel track up to the left as the road bends off to the right. Gently ascend past more vineyards off to the left and arrive at a T-junction with a **stone ruin** on the right. Turn left onto a concrete track. As the track turns sharp right, continue straight ahead towards woodland. After 50 metres take the waymarked path straight on into the woods.

Continue for 1km, crossing several streams, until you reach a small break in the woodland. Turn left uphill to a T-junction, then turn left again. At the next crossroads of tracks go downhill to the left and round the bend for startling views of the Corbières Massif limestone range.

After 500 metres join another track coming from the right and continue downhill to the left, vineyards either side. After a further 1km join another track coming from the right, again turning left onto it. On arriving at a group of cypress trees, continue on the track. At a second group, go to the right on a smaller track, turning off the main track which sweeps to the left. You soon come to the D205 again, with a **picnic table** under a tree on the left. Turn right here and enter the hamlet of **Embres-et-Castelmaure**. ◄

A small winemaking village with a working winery at its centre, there is a tap but no other shop or amenities.

Follow the road through the winding village until you come to Chemin de la Fontaine, passing the broad façade of the village wine processing unit. ◄ Continue out of the village along Chemin de la Fontaine. After 200 metres reach a fork and stay on the principal lane to the left. Begin to climb, remaining on the tarmac lane and ignoring any side turnings.

The drinkable-water tap is down to the left in front of the library.

Reach the top of the col after 1km and then descend on the lane for 800 metres to a fork. Take the right turning and cross over a concrete bridge, leaving the tarmac behind. Ignore two driveways to the right immediately after the bridge and continue on the main gravel track.

Reach a fork with a **stone building** alongside it and walk around the building to the left, with thin forest also on the left-hand side. At a fork with a lone pine tree at the centre, turn right. After 500 metres turn left at another fork onto a forestry track. Follow this gradual, easy climb for 1.2km and enjoy the wide views of the valley and limestone range.

At the **col** and the meeting of many tracks, take the footpath straight ahead, marked with a large waymarked rock. Follow the narrow footpath downhill into sparse woodland to reach a T-junction. Turn left and continue downhill, ignoring the track off to the left, and ford a (usually) dry stream bed in the valley bottom.

Shortly after, at a stony fork, turn left uphill. It makes a gentle zigzag, passing a 'Forêt Domaniale des Corbières Orientales' board on the right. After 1km take the waymarked path to the right that goes down into further forest. ▶

The route wanders in and out of two little valleys on a rocky path. After the second valley, climb a small hill and then descend into the valley of Nouvelle. Upon reaching a fenced vineyard go down the left-hand side to a metal gate. ▶

Once through the gate, continue downhill to another vineyard and again walk down the left-hand side. At a fork take the grassy track to the left into another vineyard. Walk a short distance to the right and take a turning more or less to the right, down to the road.

You are now on the outskirts of the hamlet of **Nouvelle**. Instead of going through it the Cathar Way follows the road for 1.5km through vineyards before turning left across a bridge. Follow this road, with Aguilar Castle now directly ahead. Off to the left is the ruin of Château de Domneuve with its lone cloud pine.

Follow the tarmac lane for 500 metres through more vineyards to arrive at a fork. Take the right turning, and shortly afterwards at the next fork go left. Beyond a group

Here you will get your first sight of Aguilar Castle, the first Cathar castle on the trail. If it's clear you will also see the Pyrenees beyond.

The stubby fences bordering the vines are to keep the wild boar out of the Nouvelle vineyards.

Path to Aguilar Castle

of cypress trees take the left fork uphill. At the top of the climb, round the bend for sweeping views of **Aguilar Castle** standing tall above the rafts of vineyards around. Follow the track down to the tarmac road, turning left to explore the castle.

To continue on the route, follow the tarmac road downhill for 200 metres. Just after some **picnic benches** turn left off the road onto a footpath which serves as a useful shortcut downhill. When the footpath rejoins the

AGUILAR CASTLE

The first avowed 'Cathar' castle on the Cathar Way, Aguilar Castle sits at over 300m above the surrounding vineyards, with the steep 878m Montagne de Tauch behind. There's evidence that this site has been occupied since Roman times, but the castle itself has been in existence since the 11th century, passing into the possession of the de Termes family (owners of Termes Castle) from the Trencavel counts certainly by the beginning of the Albigensian Crusade in the early 13th century.

Raymond de Termes supported the Cathars, so when Termes Castle fell to Simon de Montfort in 1210, Aguilar was also seized without resistance. Raymond's son Olivier de Termes was seemingly back in control of Aguilar by 1240, but the castle soon fell once again under French control. By 1250 Olivier de Termes had become an ally of the French Crown, and the castle was restored back to him. Olivier eventually and finally sold Aguilar Castle to the Crown for good in 1260.

Aguilar Castle was then extensively redeveloped to become one of the 'five sons of Carcassonne' (along with the castles of Puilaurens, Peyrepertuse, Quéribus and Termes) and was used to defend the new southern border of France.

After the 16th century Aguilar Castle fell out of use and, as the local tourism website says, 'was left to face the bitter Cers winds alone…' A lonesome ruin today, it is open to the public year-round.

---

tarmac road, turn left and follow the road for 1km, now on the flat through vines and trees. At an olive grove, turn left again.

After 400 metres the route joins the **D39 road**, which turns right and crosses a bridge over a stream. Continue to the outskirts of **Tuchan** and at a T-junction turn left onto the **D611** into town.

Tuchan is a pretty winemaking town with medieval defensive roots. A lot of the inhabitants today work the vines that surround it, which are run in large part as a cooperative. Tuchan also has a proud rugby tradition.

There are a fair few *chambres d'hôtes* options to choose from in Tuchan, along with a café-bar, a restaurant, post office, and that all-important grocery shop.

The ancient village and vineyards of Tuchan

STAGE 3

Tuchan to Cucugnan

Start	D611 road in Tuchan
Finish	D14 into Cucugnan
Distance	18km
Ascent	790m
Descent	650m
Time	5hr (or 6hr including visit to Quéribus Castle)
Refreshments	Padern has a restaurant and one café (with unreliable hours); Quéribus Castle has a small ticket office with a basic coffee machine; Cucugnan has several restaurants and a shop
Public transport	Bus 408 from Narbonne and Durban-Corbières serves Tuchan

This stage comprises a rewarding, moderate walk that traverses valleys and gorges and passes one of the most famous Cathar strongholds – Quéribus Castle.

Beginning in the vine-covered, sun-baked valley beyond Tuchan, the route plunges into the steep-sided rocky pass of Grau du Padern and on to the village of Padern itself with its own dramatic medieval castle. Continuing along, the view of Quéribus Castle from this stage is spectacular and the castle is really worth a diversion.

It is also worth noting that while the walking is flatter and easier than on the previous stages, it is quite exposed with little shade, making it tougher in hot weather.

Follow the D611 road south out of **Tuchan**. Outside of the village, take a footpath to the right beside the wall of a **cemetery**. After 200 metres, as the lane bends to the right, take the track hugging a stone wall that goes straight on. Another 200 metres further on, meet a fork and go right along a rocky path. Views of the vineyards and the limestone landscape open out gracefully to the left as you walk.

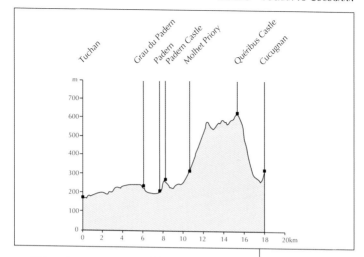

This path soon narrows and bends to the left near a house, meeting the driveway. Turn left, and after 100 metres at a meeting of tracks head straight on, crossing a concrete irrigation ditch as you go. At a bend of a small road, go right along it under a power line. Ignore side turnings to vineyards and stay on this track for 600 metres until you reach a T-junction at the corner of a vineyard. Turn left, ignoring the immediate rocky track to the right, and carry on straight down to the **D14 road**.

Turn right at the road and follow it over a bridge. After 500 metres, directly after a **stone ruin** with trees sprouting from it, turn right off the road onto a track up into the stony hillside. ▸ After 150 metres, at a fork, take the left turning. The track bends to the left and then to the right, now tarmacked. Continue straight on it, following the waymark on the post. The route now borders vines, and soon skirts around the perimeter of a large fenced vineyard. After this small diversion, reach a track and turn right.

Walk through a small ravine and on to another. There used to be a path straight across here, but since it was destroyed the route now winds in and out of the ravine.

This area is tinder-dry and can be affected by forest fires in the summer – you might see evidence of previous burnings in the vegetation on the hillsides.

47

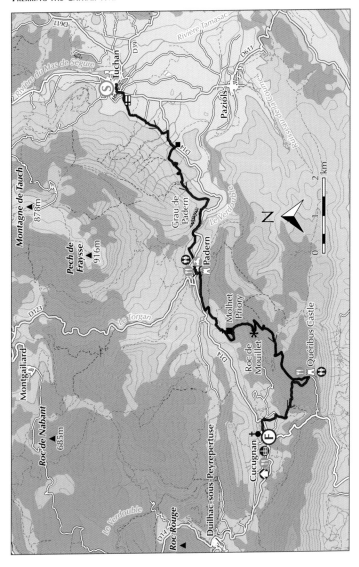

Beyond the ravines, follow the path across the hillside through Mediterranean vegetation, leaving the vineyards behind for now. After almost 1km turn sharp right around a rocky outcrop where the magnificent rocky cleft of **Grau du Padern** is revealed.

Walk into what is essentially a small gorge on an easy rocky path, gradually descending. Below is the beautifully blue River Verdouble and the winding D14 road. Pass a stone ruin on the right and meet the road and a modern Cathar Way sign. Follow the road to the right for 200 metres and turn off it just before the bridge, following a track slightly downhill. Soon you reach a clearing and a fork: turn right alongside the clearing and when it ends go straight on, taking the footpath through a parched forest of bamboo.

After 120 metres come to a track and turn left onto it. Round the bend for a view of Padern Castle perched on a rocky outcrop above the village. Continue straight on as the track becomes tarmac, reaching the wooden footbridge down on the left across the wide length of the river. Cross the footbridge and turn right to enter the village of **Padern**. ▶

In the village, follow the narrow, cobbled path round the small church. There's a sign for the 'Château' on the wall (but ignore the steps to the left of the sign). At the top of the path turn left on a small tarmac lane. After 20 metres turn right up a cobbled flight of steps, and after a further 30 metres the steps lead to a lane: continue straight on up and turn left at a chapel.

At the end of this lane take a sharp right after the cattle grid and follow a grassy path up the hillside. This footpath leads steeply to the outside of **Padern Castle**. It isn't that easy, and as the castle itself is not open to the public, exploring this route is not particularly encouraged.

The imposing keep of **Padern Castle** is perched directly above Padern village and the wide River Verdouble. Not much connects Padern with the Cathars, although *faidits* (dispossessed knights) from the south did appear to try and use it as a refuge

There is a small café across the road in Placette de l'Église; or turn left up the road for the water tap, a restaurant (La p'tite Ardoise) and public toilets.

Views towards Cucugnan and Peyrepertuse Castle

at the time of the Albigensian Crusade. The ruins today only date back to the 17th century, despite it looking much older. Padern Castle isn't open to the public.

Go down the main track, which offers a burgeoning view of a new valley. You also get the first distant view ahead of Peyrepertuse Castle. Reach another track at the bottom of the hill and join it by heading left uphill. Follow the track as it bends to the left into a small side valley, and then right.

Above and slightly to the left you will see the remains of the medieval Molhet Priory, half-consumed by vegetation.

At a staggered crossroads go right. After this, ignore a grassy turning to the left by a vineyard and instead turn left on a gravel track beyond the vines. ◀ Start to ascend on the gravel track and pass a small stone hut on the left, fringed with cypress trees. When the gravel track finishes, carry on straight along the footpath. Walk through the brush and reach the other side of **Molhet Priory**.

This plateau is Roc de Mouillet – a good spot to take a break and enjoy the view of Cucugnan, Peyrepertuse Castle and the valley.

Continue to climb onto the limestone outcrop over to the right. Around 700 metres beyond the priory the winding path meets a forestry track. Join it and continue climbing for a couple of hundred metres until you arrive at a grassy plateau on top of the limestone cliff. ◀

Continue up the forest track for another 750 metres to reach the top. When it eventually levels out, pass round the cattle grid and descend a little. Look out for the first view of the stout Quéribus Castle off to the right.

Soon after the cattle grid, turn right on the track. After 300 metres, at a fork, take the right rocky path downhill with Quéribus now ahead. Descend to a more established track and follow it to the right. Follow the gravel track as it bends sharply to the left (the track off to the right here is another route down to the village of Cucugnan).

Stay on the track as it traverses the hillside until you reach **Quéribus Castle**. There are toilets here and the ticket office has coffee and snack vending machines.

QUÉRIBUS CASTLE

An incredibly impressive sight with its distinctive polygonal keep, Quéribus Castle sits on a 728m rocky outcrop of the Corbières Massif. It was known as a formidable fortress and popularly as the last Cathar stronghold.

During the crusade Quéribus was under the sponsorship of southern lord Chabert de Barbaira, a committed defender of the Cathars. The castle actively resisted the French forces long into the middle of the 13th century, even after the fall of Montségur in 1244. When the castle was finally forced to surrender around 1255 (Barbaira is said to have been captured by former ally Olivier de Termes), the Cathar garrison living there escaped, and Barbaira himself was spared too.

The rocky approach to Quéribus Castle

After 1258 it was refortified to guard the new French frontier with Aragon and it became known as one of the 'five sons of Carcassonne' (with the castles of Aguilar, Peyrepertuse, Puilaurens and Termes).

The Quéribus of today is built of layers of fortification from the 11th–16th centuries, with most of its interior actually built within the rock. The castle is open every day and year-round, but can be closed in windy conditions. At the entrance there are basic facilities.

The keep of Quéribus Castle catching the dawn

After visiting the castle, walk up through the car park to begin descending to Cucugnan. (There's a fork at the top of the car park but both paths soon rejoin.)

The 2km route down is signposted as difficult, and after a short flat section the descent is indeed quite steep in places, but no trickier than elsewhere on the trail. There are good footholds and it's clearly waymarked. It would be dangerous in very wet weather though, so if it's raining hard it might be preferable to follow the road down from the castle car park instead.

On reaching the valley bottom turn right along a gravel track. This track continues to descend and crosses a stream, then rises to a copse of cypress trees where you turn left onto a tarmacked lane. Follow the lane, ignoring a left turn, until you reach a T-junction. Turn left and immediately reach the D14. Cross over the road and head uphill into the lovely village of **Cucugnan**.

Here there are two options: stay in Cucugnan for a range of accommodation and food options, or carry on to the village of Duilhac which also has accommodation. The latter adds 4km to the day and is described in the next stage of this book.

CUCUGNAN

A honey-hued hill village once again surrounded by vineyards, Cucugnan is now something of a tourist hub due in part to its proximity to Quéribus Castle. It also has its own 14th-century church, a hanging rose garden that is open daily, and a restored working windmill at the very top of the village.

The restored windmill at the top of Cucugnan village

Cucugnan is famously featured in an Occitan story retold in French by 19th-century writer Alphonse Daudet. It retells a fiery sermon given by the Cucugnan *curé* (priest) where he recounts a trip to hell and sees his wayward and sinful congregation consumed in the flames. Cucugnan's theatre is named after the Occitan writer of the story, Achille Mir.

There are a few restaurants in Cucugnan, as well as shops selling food, local wines and crafts, a bakery annexed to the windmill, and a choice of hotels too.

STAGE 4
Cucugnan to Saint-Paul-de-Fenouillet

Start	Cucugnan main street
Finish	Place de la République, Saint-Paul-de-Fenouillet
Distance	23.5km (or 27.5km including visit to Peyrepertuse Castle)
Ascent	1110m (or 1330m including visit to castle)
Descent	1150m (or 1370m including visit to Peyrepertuse Castle)
Time	7hr (or 9hr including visit to castle)
Refreshments	Duilhac has a couple of cafés, hotels and a small food shop, and there is a mill restaurant and a roadside café at either end of the Galamus Gorge. Saint-Paul-de-Fenouillet has cafés, restaurants and shops.
Public transport	Bus 100 runs between Saint-Paul and Perpignan and Quillan

This is a breathtaking but undeniably arduous stage, offering the chance to visit the mighty Peyrepertuse Castle before taking in the summit of a 940m mountain and then dropping into the Galamus Gorge. With that elevation, distance, and assuming the extra kilometrage to visit Peyrepertuse, this is the hardest day on the Cathar Way.

These challenges are partly due to two recent changes to the route: firstly, the ascent over the mountain directly after Pla de Brézou, which is scenic but long and steep (although this can and should be avoided in bad weather). Secondly, a sizeable diversion after the Galamus Gorge where, after the destruction of a footbridge in 2014, the Cathar Way was rerouted down to the town of Saint-Paul-de-Fenouillet. This latter change is supposedly temporary, so included below are the instructions for the old route as well, which takes you to Prugnanes – a small village near to where the Cathar Way continues in the next stage.

It is on Stage 4 that the Cathar Way splits into its two variants – 16km in, just before the Galamus Gorge. If you're continuing on the main route, note that the signage will change to GR367A until the two variants meet up again at Coudons (Stage 8).

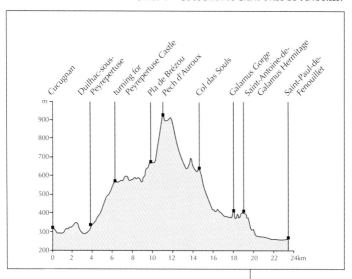

Head straight through the village of **Cucugnan** down its main road. It sweeps down to the tourist information office on a T-junction. Turn right to follow the D14, but after 50 metres, at the village end sign, fork right off the road.

About 150 metres later, ignoring the driveway up to the yard of Château Trillol, continue straight along the valley bottom, with vineyards all around. At the next fork, go right and continue until the tarmac peters out. Ignore the tracks off to the right, and you'll soon pass a small stone building on the left. As the route bends sharply to the left to rejoin the D14, turn right on a stony track. After a further 50 metres, follow the track round to the left.

Descend a rocky little slope to a T-junction and turn right down a waymarked track. There are great views here of Duilhac-sous-Peyrepertuse with Peyrepertuse Castle perched high above. Follow the track for 400 metres and turn right at a T-junction. The track bends to the left and goes downhill to arrive just beyond a vineyard. Bear left over a stream 60 metres later.

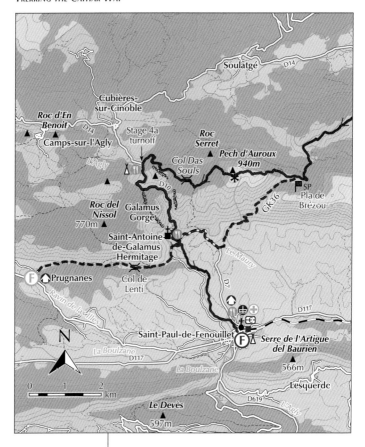

Shortly after, go straight over a staggered crossing of tarmac lanes, with another lane soon joining from the left. Carry on straight, bearing left around the hill. Fork left up a narrower lane, where a small climb begins.

At another fork 120 metres along this narrow lane, go left up the rocky footpath. This weaves uphill to the D14 once again – ignore the footpath off to the right on the way up. At the road, turn right and walk along

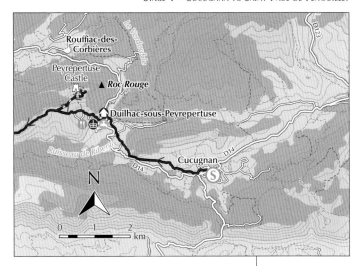

to Rue de la Fontaine, into the charming **Duilhac-sous-Peyrepertuse**. The route passes between Hostellerie di Vieux Moulin and Auberge du Moulin – you'll see the mill grinder on the wall. ▶

Walk up the road into the village centre, passing through to the pretty Place de la Forge and then Place de l'Église. Here you will find Le Fort (the fortress gates) and a water tap. Follow the waymarks through the village, passing a small shop (*épicerie*) to meet the main tarmac road leading up to the castle. Turn right onto this.

Go past a tennis and a pétanque court, and after the road bends to the left, turn right onto a stony footpath uphill. Climb through woodland for 400 metres to meet a fork. Take the right for a steep way up to Peyrepertuse Castle, or go left for the Cathar Way, off which there is an easier route up to the castle later.

Climb through the brush and arrive quickly at a clearing. Skirt the left edge to rejoin the road, and continue to follow it uphill. In 500 metres reach a sharp bend in the road to the right. From here it's 2km off the Cathar Way up the steep road to the ticket office for **Peyrepertuse Castle**.

As well as a potential alternative place to stay, Duilhac is a good stop before heading off into the wilds for the next section.

57

PEYREPERTUSE CASTLE

A wonder of medieval architecture, Peyrepertuse Castle is a breathtaking sight, floating as it does high above the valley floor, earning the nickname 'Celestial Carcassonne'. Thought to derive its actual name from the Occitan for 'pierced rock', its long walls stretch over 300 metres along the high lime-stone cliffs, and it was long seen as an impregnable fortress.

Peyrepertuse Castle from its highest chamber with the village of Duilhac-sous-Peyrepertuse below

At the time of the crusade, Peyrepertuse was controlled by southern lord Guilhem de Peyrepertuse and, although briefly surrendered, it was not captured in the early years of the campaign. Eventually, however, in 1240, after an unsuccessful attempt by southern forces to take back Carcassonne, French troops laid siege to Peyrepertuse and Guilhem de Peyrepertuse was obliged to surrender the castle.

Like other Cathar castles, it was then used by the French to bolster the border with Spain, adding more of the impressive outer walls we see today.

Inside Peyrepertuse is a fascinating crumbling complex of chambers, staircases and walkways sprawled along the knife-edge cliff. From its highest chamber there are outstanding views of Quéribus Castle and out towards the Mediterranean. The castle is open to the public year-round – but watch out for ferocious mountain gusts.

After visiting the castle, retrace your steps to the sharp bend in the road. Continue on the Cathar Way by leaving the road and following the dirt track uphill. After 250 metres the track levels out; continue for 2km, terracing along the valley side.

Round the head of the valley, and as the track curves to the left take the waymarked footpath forking off to the right. Continue along a terrace again and after 600 metres meet a forest track. Cross straight over and follow the path towards a concrete animal trough.

Join the rocky path as it veins uphill through woodland. After 400 metres, at a fork, take either turning (they join up), and 200 metres later come to the grassy, flat **Pla de Brézou**. Shaded with trees, it's a good lunch stop.

This is where the first of the two recent changes to the route begins. If the weather is fine, and to continue along the official Cathar Way, go north along the dirt footpath as signposted. Although the views on the path are magnificent, it's not for the fainthearted: it climbs very steeply and is at times precariously close to the cliff edge. It's not recommended in wet weather.

Tranquil high pasture beyond Peyrepertuse Castle

Nearing the top of Pech d'Auroux with the vast Corbières landscape below

Bad-weather alternative

The alternative is to take the GR36 from the plateau straight down the valley, heading west. This is another long-distance path, providing a waymarked and slightly shorter option, descending to just south of the Galamus Gorge where it's easy to follow the road into the gorge and pick up the Cathar Way again – incidentally, the north variant begins at the northern end of the gorge.

From the plateau, take the right footpath into the brush, climbing gradually at first. The path soon becomes steep, and for short sections you might need to use your hands to help yourself over exposed rock as you head higher and higher. Take extra care on narrow sections of path near the cliff edge. It is clearly waymarked throughout.

Climb for 1.3km from the plateau, the last 500 metres being the steepest. At the top you reach **Pech d'Auroux**, a truly extraordinary bird's-eye **view** over the vast blanket of the Corbières.

From the top, follow the fairly flat route through woodland and some open areas for almost 1km before descending steadily for another 1.3km to reach a T-junction. Turn right and climb gradually again through woodland for 500 metres to **Col das Souls**.

At a fork in the woods, go right as waymarked. A little further on ignore a very steep descent down a path to the Galamus Gorge on the left; instead stay on the balcony path to enjoy views down to the gorge and the dramatic road passing through it.

Arriving at a clearing, take the smaller track straight ahead and downhill. The path soon crosses purplish rocks before heading back into woodland. At a three-way junction in the woods take the left path and continue zigzagging gradually downhill. At a fork further below, keep twisting to the right. Once out of the woods, continue down through dry vegetation. At a T-junction in earshot of the road, turn right, still going downhill, to reach the road just outside of the gorge. ▸

There's an old mill which has a restaurant and campsite in high season.

Here the Cathar Way meets the GR36, and the north variant of the Cathar Way begins, turning right. **Turn to Stage 4a to follow that route from here.** To stay on the main (south) route, turn left along the road to the **Galamus Gorge**. Note that from here you will be following the GR367A on signposts until Coudons (Stage 8).

A narrow, 400m-deep *défilé* carved into limestone by the chalky blue River Agly, the **Galamus Gorge** is one of the most dramatic natural sights on the Cathar Way, popular with tourists and walkers alike.

Following the high road through the Galamus Gorge

Continue on the road as it hugs the high eastern side of the narrow gorge. After 3km the road emerges at the southernmost end, where there is a car park and small café. From here you can look back and spot the remarkable Franciscan **Saint-Antoine de Galamus Hermitage** clinging to the rockface at the mouth of the gorge. (It can be reached via a small footpath from the car park, and its chapel, a little grotto literally hewn out of the rock, is open daily from April to October.)

Carry on along the road for another 300 metres before turning off onto a stony footpath going downhill to the right into woodland.

A significant diversion has been created from this point after a flash flood damaged the bridge over the River Agly. There is a notice shortly after the turning, with a map detailing the diversion. If the original route has reopened, it's another 500 metres to the river crossing, and a further 4.5km to get to Prugnanes, where there is a *gîte d'étape*. Otherwise, the new route leads in 3.4km to Saint-Paul-de-Fenouillet, which is anyhow a very convenient place to finish the stage.

Either way, after 300 metres, look out for the footpath on the right signposted to Gîte Benjamin and continue down it until you reach a fork with a bench.

The Saint-Antoine Hermitage at the southern end of the Galamus Gorge

The original Cathar Way

At the bench, turn right to reach the offending character, the River Agly. Cross the river and turn left up a wide track. At the top of a hill, turn right onto a little jeep track. As this track bends left, continue straight on and onto a footpath into woodland. Climb steeply to reach a T-junction at the **Col de Lenti**, where you turn right. Almost immediately, take the path going off to the left, which descends and meets a track onto which you turn right. This eventually reaches **Prugnanes**.

From Prugnanes it's 1km back along the rough road you have already walked, to the left turning that is (currently) the official Cathar Way route – see Stage 5.

The official (diverted) Cathar Way

At the bench, turn left and continue along the small footpath until you reach a T-junction. Turn right and descend to a track. Go left along the track and continue as the lane becomes tarmacked.

Just before the lane rises to join the D7 road, turn right under a railway line and follow the track for 150 metres to then join the D7 there instead.

Turn right and follow the road round to the left, and take the second road on the right down to Place de la République in **Saint-Paul-de-Fenouillet**.

SAINT-PAUL-DE-FENOUILLET

Saint-Paul is the largest town on the route before Foix at the trail end. It looks at first glance like any other modern working place, but it has an ancient history: originally a Roman town, at its centre is the *chapitre* – a Benedictine collegiate church originally founded in the eighth century, with a distinctive 17th-century hexagonal spire. It now houses its own small archaeological museum. The parish church of St Peter and St Paul is originally 11th century, rebuilt in the 14th.

It does also offer the walker precious amenities on what is otherwise quite an isolated stage, with shops including a choice of supermarkets, a pharmacy, bar-cafés, hotels, and a bank.

STAGE 5

Saint-Paul-de-Fenouillet to Caudiès-de-Fenouillèdes

Start	Place de la République, Saint-Paul-de-Fenouillet
Finish	Village shop, Caudiès-de-Fenouillèdes
Distance	22km (or 13.5km via lower-level alternative)
Ascent	930m (or 460m via lower-level alternative)
Descent	840m (or 370m via lower-level alternative)
Time	7hr (or 4hr via lower-level alternative)
Refreshments	There is a remote possibility the Prugnanes *gîte d'étape* will be open for food or drink, but there are no other places to buy food until Caudiès
Public transport	Bus 500 from either Quillan or Perpignan to Saint-Paul-de-Fenouillet, plus also the 'Red' tourist train links Perpignan to Axat

Decisions about the route need to be made today, as the trail splits again. After continuing for a time on a fairly easy gravel path through a lush wooded valley, the official route goes off up to higher plateaux and the remote ruin of Campeau, adding much in both beauty and difficulty. There is an alternative: an ancient route stays lower along a less interesting lane, but saving around 9km and about 500m in ascent in comparison to the official route. Both meet up in Caudiès-de-Fenouillèdes.

Either way refreshment options are virtually non-existent, so take all the food and fluids necessary for the day.

From Place de la République in the centre of **Saint-Paul-de-Fenouillet**, go down Rue Arago, signposted to the *mairie* (town hall). Follow the road to its end and through Place Florentin Pla.

Turn right onto the D117, cross over the River Agly and take the first right after the bridge. Continue for 700 metres, cross over the train tracks and immediately turn left to follow a gravel track out into Languedoc countryside. After a further 600 metres, at the corner of a

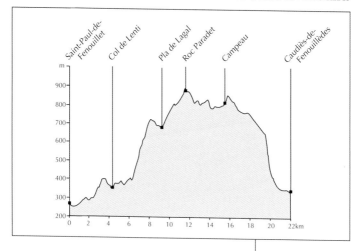

vineyard, keep right – don't go left into it. Continue for 500 metres, and as a track joins from the right, continue straight on, going slightly uphill to the left. Soon after, at a fork, turn left, passing a waymark on a post. Around 400 metres later, at another fork, turn right to leave the principal track.

Ascend beside the vine rows to a narrow gap in the bushes. Step through and continue uphill into sparse woodland. The path levels out for a short distance, descends into a little valley, then climbs out again on a section that is steep and rocky in places. The path then flattens and skirts round the east side of a hill. Continue along an overgrown path to eventually come out at a track crossroads at the **Col de Lenti**. Turn left here. ▶

After 300 metres keep right at a fork. As a new valley appears ahead, join a track and follow it to the right, continuing on it for 2km towards Prugnanes. But before you reach the village a signpost directs you off the track, pointing you up the hillside.

Here there is the choice previously described: the newer official Cathar Way, or the lower-level (and quicker) ancient route. If choosing the official route,

A path joins here from the right – this is the original Cathar Way route that crossed over the River Agly. The diversion that started in the previous stage has now ended.

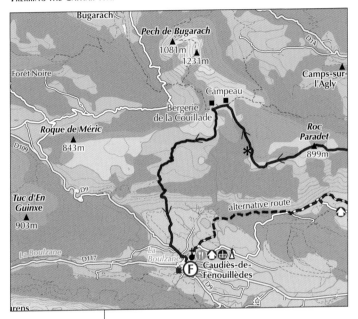

continue reading; if following the ancient route, skip down to the alternative route notes below.

Official route to Caudiès-de-Fenouillèdes

Turn right up the hillside and begin the fairly steep ascent through the brush. Zigzag up a loose rocky path for just under 1km, continuing the climb through scrubby woodland. Shortly beyond a very small clearing turn left at a fork, signposted towards Camps-sur-l'Agly and Paradet. (The right fork goes to the Galamus Gorge passed through in Stage 4.)

After another 300 metres of climbing in and out of woodland, turn left onto a more established track coming from Col de Lenti. Immediately after joining the track, fork right onto the main and more obvious way. Shortly after climbing some more, walk straight across a grassy clearing, picking up a jeep track. In the woodland beyond,

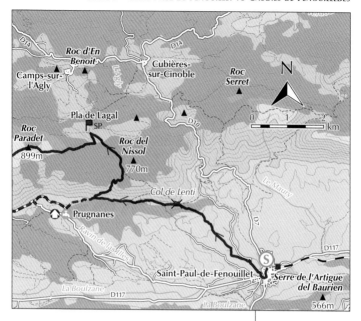

fork right, signposted to Camps-sur-l'Agly (ignore the left
fork signposted to Paradet).

Continue out onto an open plateau, with high hilltop
views all around. The jeep track heads through juniper
bushes to a junction signposted to **Pla de Lagal**, a flat
highland area. Turn left and begin a gentle but long climb
to the next plateau.

The climb continues on the jeep track but soon leaves
the clearing to enter woodland. Shortly after entering the
woods a path joins from the left (the left fork signposted to
Paradet previously). Continue for just over 2km, following
the main track through woodland and out into high pasture at **Roc Paradet**, the 900m highpoint of the stage. ▶

Start descending from Roc Paradet and after 100
metres fork left, then almost immediately fork again to
the left, away from the jeep track and onto a minor path.
Cross this plateau, following the squat little cairns.

There are brilliant
views, including of
Pech de Bugarach
to the northwest.

Continue walking steadily downhill, contouring the high pasture and enjoying the excellent views of the valley that is crossed on the Cathar Way later in the stage. The little path leads eventually into a wooded valley where there's a fork. Take the right, signposted to Campeau. (The left route is a very steep way down to Prugnanes, but a little way along it there are a series of quite impressive caves which can be explored.)

Continuing towards Campeau, the wooded path climbs steadily and reaches a rocky clearing strewn with lavender and yellowing grasses. Cross straight over it, following more cairns – take care as they are a little hard to spot. The path ducks into undergrowth and up to an outstanding **viewpoint** where you get another good angle of the Pech de Bugarach.

The path then descends in and out of woodland over rocky and rooted ground. Upon reaching obvious pasture to the left, descend to the shallow valley floor, following waymarks on rocks and trees. Then enjoy the gentle walk uphill toward the centre of the pasture for a couple of hundred metres before turning onto a woodland path.

The Pech de Bugarach

This path is very old, and although more often used these days by the free-roaming cattle up on the pasture, it was once an important **access route** for the now ruined settlement at Campeau.

After a time, the path becomes less wooded and eventually just follows an avenue of trees. Pass an artificial lake on the left to arrive at the abandoned village and farmstead of **Campeau**. ▸

Stage 5a of the north variant of the Cathar Way joins for a short way here.

With the lake on the left and the buildings on the right, walk uphill following the waymarks. At a large open field with the gargantuan Pech de Bugarach to the right, the path continues across the pasture and through the copse in the middle, waymarked on small fence posts and little cairns. At the top right corner of the field you'll arrive at the ruins of **Bergerie de la Couillade** (an old sheepfold) and another signpost. ▸

The trail divides here, with the north variant turning right and this stage going left.

Continue along the tree-lined edge of the pasture and descend on a clear rough track. Bear right and cross an open plateau and continue walking through this beautiful upland area. After 2km from Bergerie de la Couillade, turn left onto a grassy jeep track, which then winds gently downhill.

Continue for some time over very peaceful pastureland and eventually you'll come to a signpost to Bergerie de Malabrac (another sheepfold). Turn left here. The track continues to descend, bearing right between box trees. At a shady T-junction, turn left. Downhill all the way, continue to a waymarked right turn into the woods; take this and then another left to reach semi-open ground, levelling out once more.

After passing an old well on the right, re-enter a patch of woodland and the descent begins in earnest. The next few kilometres down to Caudiès-de-Fenouillèdes are very steep, clambering over bare rock and passing through bits of sparse woodland. ▸

Be careful of loose stones and slippery leaflitter – use them as an excuse to take your time and admire the incredible view of Caudiès far below.

Pay attention to the waymarks zigzagging downwards, particularly at two ravine crossings. Eventually the gradient eases and the path is enveloped in evergreen oak woodland. After some time you'll emerge onto open ground and eventually join a lane on the edge of vineyards.

Follow the lane to meet the **D9** and turn left towards **Caudiès-de-Fenouillèdes**. Cross the bridge over the Boulzane and follow the D9 uphill into the village centre. Continue on to the D117, the road with the village shop.

A formerly fortified town, **Caudiès-de-Fenouillèdes** is clustered around a central square framed by half-timber houses, a 17th-century parish church and what was once its own castle, Castel Fizel.

The town is also a useful stop-off as it has several different types of accommodation, including a hotel and a campsite. There are also multiple shops, including a food shop, a pharmacy, a restaurant, and a café-bar.

Lower-level alternative from Prugnanes to Caudiès-de-Fenouillèdes

Continue down on the track into the hamlet of **Prugnanes**, where there is a water tap. At a T-junction with the *gîte d'étape* on the left, turn right

Follow this lane for 1km through vineyards and small-holdings to reach the D20. Turn right on this road, follow it up to a col and take a track off to the right. This soon becomes a pleasant balcony route overlooking a newly forested part of the main valley.

The terracotta-coloured streets of Prugnanes on the alternative route to Caudiès-de-Fenouillèdes

Follow this route as it gradually descends. After 1km ignore a track back down to the left and continue straight on, up into pine forest. After another 1km arrive at a track junction: go straight on, slightly to the right, and begin to descend.

After a further 400 metres ignore the track up to the right and continue straight on downhill. The path soon s-bends and gradually curls to the right, revealing the village of Caudiès-de-Fenouillèdes. Keep following the main track as it works its way through vineyards and arable fields to meet the D20. Turn right and follow the road alongside a stream towards the village. Cross a bridge over the Boulzane to enter **Caudiès-de-Fenouillèdes**. Follow the D20 uphill to the left to meet the D117 and to find the village shop.

STAGE 6

Caudiès-de-Fenouillèdes to Axat

Start	D117 in the centre of Caudiès-de-Fenouillèdes
Finish	Aude River bridge, Axat
Distance	21.75km
Ascent	920m
Descent	850m
Time	6hr (or 8½hr including visits to the castles)
Refreshments	Puilaurens Castle ticket office has a shop that sells drinks (but not food)
Public transport	Bus 500 from either Quillan or Perpignan to Caudiès-de-Fenouillèdes, plus there's the 'Red' tourist train linking Perpignan to Axat which stops in Lapradelle, a 3km walk from Puilaurens Castle

Today's route meanders past two sites of Cathar interest: the twin Fenouillet ruins and the imposing Puilaurens Castle. The former are two less-trammelled Cathar castles, free to visit, perched just off the official Cathar Way route. Vastly different in terms of preservation, Puilaurens and Fenouillet are well worth seeing.

The landscape around the Cathar castles now begins to change, the open vineyards being replaced by dense forest and mountain valleys.

Axat is a convenient place to finish, with its own thriving tourist industry and a range of accommodation options. Note that if following the main (south) route to the end, this is the last place with an ATM before Foix.

Cross the D117 in **Caudiès-de-Fenouillèdes** onto the smaller D9 heading out of the village. On the outskirts, cross the railway tracks and fork right onto a narrower lane which quickly becomes a track.

Wind up the hill, ignoring a track to the right after 250 metres, and continue straight ahead to the right of some vines. At the corner of a vineyard a little further on go straight ahead, following a path into the scrub.

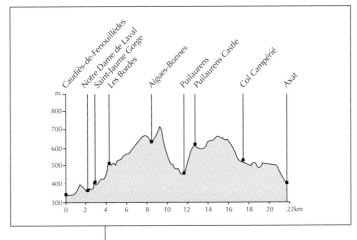

Climb steadily on a rocky footpath for 400 metres to reach a forestry track. Turn left downhill on this track and weave down to a clearing with three tracks to choose from: follow the middle option downhill as it becomes an avenue with mature trees.

Another clearing is reached after 600 metres, this time with a shady **picnic area**. ◄ Walk through the car park to the right of the picnic area and go right to meet the D9 road again.

Follow the road for 300 metres to a bridge over the river, but just before it turn right onto a footpath. Begin the gentle ascent up the Saint-Jaume Gorge.

Up to the left is the 15th-century chapel of Notre Dame de Laval, with its recently restored oak door.

The **Saint-Jaume Gorge** is a deep and narrow limestone gorge overflowing with ferns, flowers and vegetation and criss-crossed with footbridges (the pathways have handrails over the narrower parts).

Note that it is a popular breeding ground for processionary caterpillars, the non-native species steadily eating its way through the local vegetation. It's best to avoid them as they can cause a reaction like a nasty sting.

Duck beneath overhanging rocks and cross several little footbridges as you ascend the gorge. After about 1km, pass a hamlet, then a waterfall. Climb out of the gorge up the stony track and turn left at a tarmac lane. Immediately come to a crossroads.

To explore the **Fenouillet Castles**, turn left here off the Cathar Way and follow both the signposting and the red-and-white waymarks of the GR36 for about 500 metres along the tarmac lane up to the hamlet of **la Vilasse**. Once you've explored the castles, retrace your steps to the crossroads mentioned above.

Castel Sabordas and the hamlet of la Vilasse from Château Saint Pierre

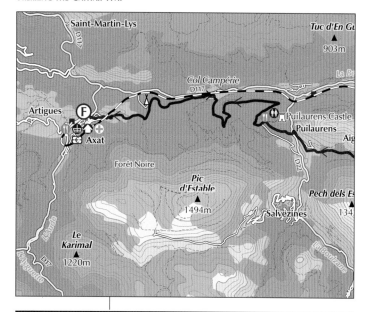

THE FENOUILLET CASTLES

Among the least-known Cathar fortresses, the two Fenouillet Castles and fortified settlement were inhabited by Cathar supporters until the middle of the 13th century. The remains of Château Saint Pierre and Castel Sabordas sit closely atop twin hills, with la Vilasse, a village that is still inhabited, between them. The two ruins are open to explore freely, with striking views of each other.

Go straight ahead at the crossroads, waymarked as the GR367. Pass between two stone buildings and stay on the lane as it sweeps left. After the bend, take a sharp right onto a grassy footpath uphill.

Climb for 200 metres and enter the hamlet of **les Bordes**. ◄ Continue straight on through the hamlet, joining the tarmac lane and turning right downhill away from the little settlement, with a good view of the Fenouillet Castles to the right.

Drinking water is signposted to the left here.

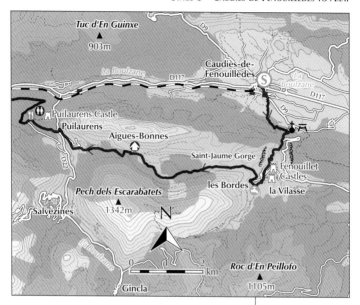

A short way down the road, turn left on the right-hand
bend, signposted GR367 to Quillan. After 600 metres
ignore a grassy track off to the right and carry straight
ahead on the main track uphill. Continue for around 250
metres, then at a fork take the right track straight on.

After 1km pass an off-grid house and smallholding.
Continue on the gently climbing track to reach another
fork and turn left. Now beginning the walk through the
Aigues-Bonnes Valley, walk for around 1.5km to reach
the *gîte d'étape* and cattle farm at **Aigues-Bonnes**.

Pass through the yard and join a tarmac lane that
skirts around the farmhouse to the left and climbs to
reach a wide layby and a large track on the left. Ignore
that track and go straight ahead on the waymarked footpath into the woods.

Climb steeply again through the trees, coming out
to a forest track. Turn right onto it, then immediately
right again onto a footpath. Descend on this peaceful

pine-tree-lined path, the lush green landscape unfurling around you. Continue downhill for 1.5km to reach a farm track. Turn right, and 400 metres further on join a tarmac lane, following it downhill to the left, where you'll see Puilaurens Castle perched on bare rock. Wind down steadily to the village of **Puilaurens**.

> **Puilaurens** sits directly below the castle along the River Boulzane. The area was an active part of the Allies' liberation campaign during World War II, with the Americans parachuting into its surrounding mountainsides in August 1944. A monument stands in nearby Salvezines as testament to the soldiers' bravery.

From the bus stop in the centre of Puilaurens, begin the climb to Puilaurens Castle. Cross the river and then the road, following Rue de Château. After 40 metres turn right onto Chemin du Château. This track climbs steeply at first out of the village, and then more gradually for 800 metres through forest to eventually come out at the car park and ticket office for **Puilaurens Castle**.

PUILAURENS CASTLE

One of the most commanding (and appealing) of the Cathar citadels, Puilaurens Castle stands at the top of a spur of 697m, watching over the pine-covered Boulzane valley. Like Quéribus, it was one of the last fortifications to fall into French hands during the crusade, surviving even after the fall of Montségur in 1244. Puilaurens was eventually surrendered for the ransom of southern leader, Chabert de Barbaira.

After the Treaty of Corbeil in 1258 it was made one of the 'five sons of Carcassonne' and extensively redesigned to defend the new French border. The oldest part of the site, dating back to before the Albigensian Crusade, is the square tower and keep. The outer walls and gates were built between the 13th and 17th centuries, and the impressive military features of chicanes, crenulations, merlons and terraces are all fine examples of defensive engineering from across the castle's history.

Puilaurens Castle

It is open every day from April until the middle of November, closing from December to March. At the ticket office you can buy drinks, snacks and souvenirs. There are public toilets here as well.

The walk up to the castle has been illustrated with signs about the local plant life, which includes: heather (*bruyère*), boxwood (*buis*), cherry tree (*cerisier*), white oak (*chêne pubescent*), holm oak (*chêne vert*), wild rose (*églantier*), blackthorn (*épine noire*), juniper (*genévrier*), and Scots pine (*pin sylvestre*).

To continue on the Cathar Way, walk through the car park by the ticket office and up the access road. After 150 metres, at a layby, take the stony track furthest to the right.

Follow this track through the forest for 4.5km as it bends to the left and right. After an initial gradual ascent it's all downhill. At another track, turn right and walk towards a bridge over a railway line. This is the **Col Campérié**. ▸

Turn left before the bridge and pass a World War II memorial commemorating a nearby air disaster. Follow the track parallel to the railway line for about 1km, still through forest. It then veers away from the railway line

Here you're crossing the narrow-gauge railway of the distinctive Train Rouge – the red tourist train that runs through the Fenouillèdes landscape from April to October.

and begins to climb. At a bend at the top of the slope, take the turning off to the right – be careful not to miss it as the forestry tracks are a little messy. Immediately ignore the downhill track to the left, carry on and at a fork take the waymarked path right.

Follow the earthen forestry track as it undulates downhill to a stream. Cross over the stream and turn left on a more established forestry track. After 300 metres pass Le Crémade **campsite** and continue straight on as a track joins from the right. Cross two streams, and at an open area turn right downhill.

Another 300 metres later, at a track fork, turn left and then after another 50 metres turn left again at another fork. At the crest of a hill the town of Axat comes into view, and lovely views of the Aude Valley. The track starts descending more steeply here.

Cross the railway line and wind down into the town centre. Follow Rue de l'Église at a crossroads, and then Rue de la Fontaine past pretty pastel-coloured houses. At the bottom of the hill cross over the River Aude into **Axat** by one of the two bridges.

> Built along the banks of the River Aude, attractive **Axat** is a terminus stop for the 'Red' tourist railway that runs between here and Rivesaltes (near Perpignan), and is a popular base for rafting and canoeing.
>
> For walkers it has all the local amenities including a boulangerie, hotels, bar, shop, pharmacy and bank machine. You may not find any other shops open until Espezel (end of Stage 9), and potentially no more ATMs either, so buy food for a few days.

STAGE 7
Axat to Quirbajou

Start	Aude River bridge, Axat
Finish	Quirbajou church
Distance	12.25km
Ascent	950m
Descent	550m
Time	5hr
Refreshments	None after Axat, including in Quirbajou
Public transport	Bus 402 links Axat with Quillan, plus also the 'Red' tourist train links Axat with Perpignan

This is a shorter stage but one that is still quite challenging due to a few steep climbs. The hard work pays off though as you pass through some impressive Pyrenean scenery, where thickly forested valleys are interspersed with pastoral farmland and studded with ancient hilltop villages.

There is a wonderful *gîte d'étape* in charming Quirbajou, but if this is unavailable there is another in nearby Labeau. For the latter, follow the alternative route directions.

There is nowhere to stop for refreshments per se, even in Quirbajou, so take advantage of the amenities in Axat and prepare for both this stage and the next to Puivert.

After crossing the river in the centre of **Axat**, turn left on the D118 and walk through the village, staying close to the river. After 300 metres fork right onto the more minor D317. Follow this road gradually uphill until the train station appears on the right, just beside the roundabout.

Take the D83 straight ahead, to the right of a former hotel. Cross over the railway bridge and follow the tarmac lane uphill for 200 metres. After the road bends to the left, take a gravel turning off the road to the right.

This track winds up above the village and eventually comes to open pasture. The track peters out into a more rugged and grassy path ascending the col slightly

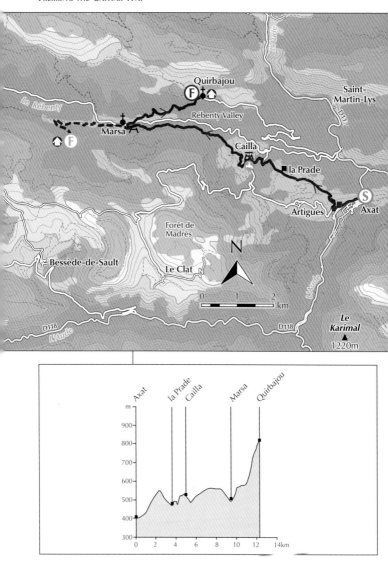

At the top of the climb out of Axat, looking back at the mountain surround

to the left between fields. At the top of this climb ignore the turning to the left signposted 'Sentier du Train'. Head straight on and slightly downhill, ignoring another path off to the right after 250 metres.

Descend gradually and then rise again to pass modern farm buildings on the left. The crumbling hamlet of **la Prade** is over to the right. ▶ At a junction of lanes overlooking la Prade, take the hamlet access lane downhill. Follow it as it becomes a track and rounds the hill into the Rébenty Valley.

> The **Rébenty River** has carved out a gorge running west–east that is surprisingly remote. Dotted with ancient villages, the Rébenty Valley is thickly forested, with even the occasional report of a bear wandering down to these hills from the Pyrenees.

The village of Cailla soon comes into view, surprisingly close. Come out onto the bend of a tarmac road with a bus stop on the right. Turn left up this road and follow it into **Cailla**. Walk towards the village and follow the tarmac lane sharply round to the left. The village centre is on the right, where there is a drinking-water tap.

La Prade is an old settlement which dates from 1150 and still farms the pigs used for the cured meats eaten in the area.

After the bend, continue to a fork in the road. To the left of the fork there is a *lavoir* (wash house) and **picnic tables** – a good place for a break. To continue, take the right-hand route downhill and pass through a yard and to the right of a farm outbuilding. Follow the small road down into valley. At a fork keep to the principal track on the right. Pass an instruction board with information on Pyrenean mountain dogs.

PYRENEAN MOUNTAIN DOGS

This part of the Pyrenees foothills is used extensively for farming livestock that are traditionally guarded by Pyrenees mountain dogs. There are several advice boards for hikers along the route, with the general gist being if you encounter one, remain calm, give the dog a wide berth, don't walk directly at it or its flock – and remember that 'they are trained not to attack, but to dissuade'.

After a further 200 metres walk through a farm and to the left as waymarked. Pass through a gate and begin a 5km journey to the village of Marsa, along a wonderful old terraced path above the Rébenty Valley.

There are good views back along the **Rébenty Valley**, especially from some pastures soon after the farm. The jagged peak visible just above Puilaurens is Serre de la Quière, standing at 1029m.

When the path meets a forestry track go straight across and downhill to enter **Marsa**, passing by its beautiful Romanesque church. Continue along Rue de l'Église to the Rébenty River bridge.

Alternative route from Marsa to Labeau (3km one-way)
If diverting off to Labeau for accommodation, do not cross the river but continue on a track on its southern bank, heading west. Continue for 1km, turning right to cross the stream. Eventually turn left onto the tarmacked road to Labeau. From here the way to the *gîte d'étape* is clear.

To continue on the main route from Marsa to Quirbajou, cross over the Rébenty River, passing Marsa's cheerful *mairie* on the left (there are also shady picnic tables here), and turn right to follow the road and river. Near the edge of the village, turn left down a grassy track towards the river. Follow the track to the left and begin the climb to Quirbajou.

This climb is 3km long with 300m ascent and has three distinct sections: the first 500 metres is steep, the next 1km is easier, and the last 1.5km is another slog. Thankfully, the views back to the now tiny Cailla, sitting serenely on a plateau with the limestone mountains behind, are wonderful. Keep ascending until eventually a smattering of smallholdings appear, heralding the outskirts of **Quirbajou**. The path leads into the heart of the village and its small church.

With its 50 inhabitants all working little plots of land, **Quirbajou** is an attractively rustic village that has a thriving communal feel. And its position high on a terrace in the mountains lends it a peaceful magnificence that few other places offer. The *gîte d'étape* on the settlement outskirts offers a place to stay and good, homecooked food. There is, however, no shop or other amenities in Quirbajou.

Looking back to Cailla from the ascent to Quirbajou

STAGE 8

Quirbajou to Puivert

Start	Quirbajou church
Finish	Place de l'Église, Puivert village
Distance	21.5km
Ascent	600m
Descent	930m
Time	6hr (or 8hr+ including visit to Puivert Castle)
Refreshments	None until Puivert
Public transport	Bus 500 from Quillan (7km off the main route using the north variant) to Perpignan or bus 402 to Carcassonne

The large and remarkably intact Puivert castle lies at the end of this stage. Once a vibrant cultural centre of Occitan music and performance, it was seized by the French forces during the crusade.

As most of the path on this stage is through woodland, and with a long descent through the forest lasting many kilometres, it's a good day for spotting wild boar or deer. And peeping over the treetops are flashes of Pyrenean mountains and rock features of the local limestone karsts.

If walking from Labeau the going isn't quite as tranquil, as the initial route up and out of the Rébenty Valley is tough.

At Coudons, around 8.5km into the stage, you will only be 7km away from the bustling town of Quillan. Coudons also being the point at which the north variant rejoins the main route, it's possible to follow the north variant in reverse from there to reach Quillan (see Stage 7a).

Alternative start from Labeau (7.5km to main route; 26km total stage length)

Walk down the Labeau access lane to the D107 and turn left. Soon after, turn right onto a path up the hillside, climbing steeply – particularly at the end – before joining a track and turning right. Walk along this high route, with views of the Plateau de Sault, to eventually rejoin the main Cathar Way. Turn left onto it and pick up the instructions where indicated below.

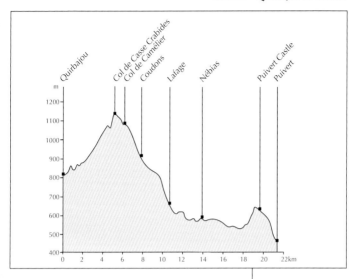

Beginning at the church in **Quirbajou**, follow Rue de la Piale through the village. This becomes Chemin du Puits (the *puits* referring to a well in a cabin on the right). Eventually the road becomes a track out of the village and through smallholdings. 600 metres from the centre of Quirbajou pass to the left of an iron cross – symbol of an ancient way – and continue alongside stone walls.

Soon after this, the track joins a larger forestry track that appears from the left, and slopes gradually uphill. Follow this track through woodland for 1.5km to reach a fork in the path. ▶ Follow the rougher track up to the right, and at another fork 400 metres later keep left, continuing uphill. After a further 500 metres a small clearing appears where you take a sharp left, as waymarked. Shortly afterwards, at another fork, turn left and the path heads steadily uphill. On the left, the peaks of the Pyrenees are visible on a clear day.

Just before the col, ignore a grassy track off to the left; keep right and follow the track along the border of a copse of pine trees. After descending slightly to a clearing, tackle

The route from Labeau joins from the left fork here.

one last ascent to reach the **Col de Casse Crabides**. Now begins a steady descent for a fair few kilometres.

Bear right and gradually descend for 1km to a T-junction at a forest clearing. Turn right and go over another col – the barely noticeable **Col de Camélier**. Zigzag down the forestry track for 2.2km, ignoring any side turnings, to reach the village of **Coudons**.

At the T-junction in Coudons, turn right. ◄ Follow the D613 road out of the village. After 200 metres, note a path off to the right: this is the route of the north variant from Quillan (Stage 7a). It is possible to leave the

There is a drinking-water tap in Coudons over to the left.

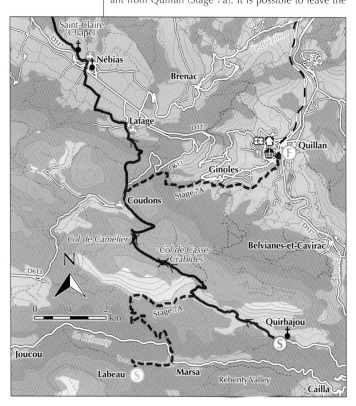

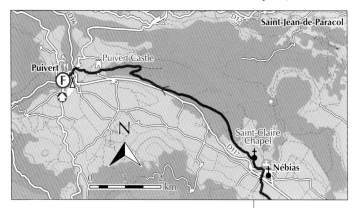

main route here and follow the north variant in reverse to access the bustling town of Quillan 7km away, where there is a bus link (Carcassone and Perpignan) and lots of accommodation.

To continue on the main route to Puivert, pass this footpath and walk along the road for 300 metres. As the road bends to the right, turn off to the left onto the tarmacked lane. When the lane swings left towards the house, take the right lane straight on, out into open farmland.

The lane soon becomes a jeep track; 400 metres further on, at a fork, take the right again, straight on, signposted as the north variant of the Cathar Way. (The route to the left is the GR7, which has come all the way from Cádiz in southern Spain.)

After a further 120 metres, ignore a left turn towards wood stacks and continue straight down a sunken lane. Some 300 metres later, at another fork, turn left onto the footpath, away from the principal track. It is waymarked with a faded cross on a rock, and another waymark on a tree a bit further on.

Follow this footpath through forest as it zigzags steeply downhill for 500 metres until you come to a crossroads on the edge of the forest. There is a vast and beautiful view of the open valley ahead. Go straight over, through a deforested plot to re-enter the forest and continue to descend on a track, following it to the right to emerge again with meadows on both sides.

Come to a T-junction and turn left, skirting the hamlet of **Lafage**. Pass to the right of a shuttered house and onto Avenue de la Croix de Simon. ◄

At this house there's a drinking-water tap under the shelter to the left.

Go downhill for 50 metres and turn left down the track between a house and allotments. This track terraces along the hillside for 1km before reaching a track

Ivy-covered cottage in Lafage

88

junction. Turn right and begin a descent to the valley base (a former lake).

When the track flattens out, come to a crossroads and turn left. After 500 metres, at another crossroads, turn right and go straight into the village of **Nébias**, crossing a stream and the D117. ▸

There's another drinking-water tap on the left.

A picturesque village with a large church and the curious feature of a fountain marking the Atlantic and Mediterranean watershed, **Nébias** is the point at which rivers to the east flow to the Mediterranean, and rivers to the west to the Atlantic.

On the outskirts of the village is the ruin of an old windmill and some labyrinthine limestone rock formations that are typical of this karst-riven area.

Unfortunately, there's currently no shop or café here.

Head straight up the Grand Rue towards the church. Pass to the left of it and come to the village square. Turn left down a tree-lined avenue and continue for 200 metres, and at a fork go right towards a small chapel along Allée de la Chapelle. ▸

The little Saint-Claire Chapel is a recently renovated 16th-century creation, said to be built on the site of an oratory known for a miraculous healing spring.

Pass by the chapel and follow this track out of the village into open countryside, with the first view of Puivert Castle in the distance. After 600 metres, at a cattle gate, take the track to the left (straight on). Keep on this path, which is well waymarked, for just over 2km, ignoring several smaller turnings off.

On reaching a crossroads, go straight over and again ignore turnings. The track becomes a footpath shortly after approaching the D117 again. You then bear away from the road and begin to climb through the sparse woodland.

After 1km, turn right onto a rocky track going uphill. This is quite a tough little climb and fairly exposed, but it's only 300 metres in length and is the last climb of the day. Reaching a T-junction at the top, turn left to descend gently to **Puivert Castle**.

PUIVERT CASTLE

Rare in the sense that it is at once intact and has strong Cathar ties, Puivert Castle was at one time a vibrant court where musicians and the roving troubadours came to perform their lyrical Occitan poetry. At the time of the crusade, the lord of Puivert, Bernard de Congost, was a Cathar – as was his wife, and his daughter Saissa de Congost – and the castle surrendered to the French army in 1210 after a short siege. Saissa de Congost was one of those burned at the stake at Montségur in 1244.

Front entrance of Puivert Castle

Although it is one of the best-preserved Cathar castles, a lot of the surviving buildings date from the 14th century – quite a bit after the Cathar period. And although a little austere on the outside, the interior of one of its chambers holds the echo of its musical past, embellished with carvings of medieval musicians and their instruments – including the bagpipes, viol, drum, lute and organ.

The castle is privately owned but open to the public year-round.

After visiting the castle, take a little footpath down to the car park. At the far end of the car park the GR7 goes off to the right, while the Cathar Way descends on the left, following the Sentier des Troubadours for a short while.

After 60 metres, at a fork, go right along Rue du Chemin du Château, which descends gradually to Puivert village. On joining a tarmac road, turn left downhill towards the centre of **Puivert**. As the lane bears to the left, carry straight on towards a collection of road signs. Emerge out onto the D117 and continue straight on to arrive at Place de la Poste. Follow the road to the right into Place de l'Église.

For somewhere to eat, stay on the D117 and follow it to the right for 100 metres, crossing a bridge, to come to a café and a pizza restaurant.

PUIVERT

Pretty Puivert village sits below the castle on a mountain meadow plain and its history is closely entwined with that of the castle. One of its oldest buildings houses the Musée du Quercorb – a museum that reconstructs scenes of medieval country life. It also exhibits copies of the sculptures of musicians and medieval musical instruments from inside Puivert Castle. The museum is open from April to September.

The land between Puivert and Nébias has a disastrous story attached to it: the whole area of almost 200 hectares used to be a large lake, but in the years after the crusade a dam gave way and drained it entirely, destroying Mirepoix downstream and much else in the valley. There's a tale that the then lord of Puivert did it for a princess, who disliked sitting by the water, but she too was swept away in the carnage. Only the wide, fertile plain is seen today.

There are a fair few accommodation options in Puivert, from *chambres d'hôtes* (B&Bs) to a campsite, as well as a restaurant and café-bar – but note there's no shop or bank, although the campsite's snack hut is open in summer.

CUCUGNAN TO PUIVERT: NORTH VARIANT

STAGE 4A
Cucugnan to Camps-sur-l'Agly

Start	Cucugnan main street (Stage 4a begins at the old mill on the D10 road just north of Galamus Gorge)
Finish	Camps-sur-l'Agly village centre
Distance	20.5km (or 24.5km including visit to Peyrepertuse Castle)
Ascent	1130m (or 1350m including castle visit)
Descent	930m (or 1150m including castle visit)
Time	6½hr (or 8½hr including visit to Peyrepertuse Castle)
Refreshments	Small restaurant in Cubières-sur-Cinoble, slightly off route

Although this first stage of the north variant is just over 20km, only the last 4km or so differs from Stage 4 of the main route. At the old mill mentioned in the latter, the north variant diverges and cuts northwest through countryside to the small settlement of Camps-sur-l'Agly.

It is the beginning of a very remote section of the Cathar Way – note that you won't see a proper shop again until Quillan, at the end of Stage 6a.

If accommodation is unavailable in Camps-sur-l'Agly, continue on for a further 2.5km to the *gîte d'étape* in la Bastide (Stage 5a).

Ahead is the Pech de Bugarach mountain ridge – a remarkable and defining feature of the north variant route.

Follow the instructions in Stage 4 until you reach the Stage 4a turnoff at the old mill on the D10. Here turn right onto the road, crossing over a car bridge marked with a red-and-white waymark. ◄

After crossing another bridge, turn sharp left off the road and onto a dirt track. (If continuing to Cubières-sur-Cinoble, stay on the road for another 300 metres). Cross a stream and then continue around the hillside, the path undulating a bit until it descends.

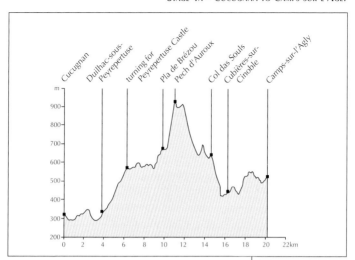

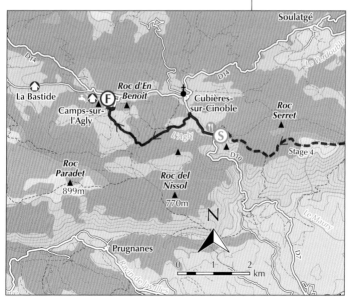

93

Approach to Camps-sur-l'Agly from the southeast

CUBIÈRES-SUR-CINOBLE

Site of a large abbey dating back to 844, now only the village church remains in Cubières-sur-Cinoble. It's also the hometown of Guilhem Bélibaste, known as the last Cathar Perfect in Languedoc. He was burned at the stake in 1321 in Villerouge-Termenès.

There is a small restaurant in Cubières that – if it chooses to open – makes a good lunch stop.

At the bottom of the hill, at a crossroads, cross the wooden footbridge over the small **River Agly** and turn right. Very soon afterwards, fork left uphill, signposted to Camps-sur-l'Agly. A long but gentle climb follows, mostly through woodland.

Near the top of the hill, fork right, signposted to Camps Bastide. Come to the top of the col and a clearing of open ground and continue straight on a grassy path. A little way on there may be a wire fence to unhook, but continue, passing a reedy lake on the left, unhooking another wire fence after. The grassy footpath gently descends in open countryside, with a glancing view of Camps-sur-l'Agly on the right.

Passing through a third wire fence, come out to a stony jeep track with a wooden signpost. Turn right and descend, crossing over a stream, before heading back up into **Camps-sur-l'Agly**. On reaching the outskirts of the village and a tarmac lane, turn left into the centre to find the accommodation.

CAMPS-SUR-L'AGLY

One of the smallest places to stay on the entire Cathar Way, this sleepy little village sits in a natural basin surrounded by beautiful mountain countryside, and near the source of the River Agly. It once had an 11th-century castle but next to nothing now remains of this, and the site became the quarry for the stone used to build the village houses.

There is only one place to stay here: the *gîte d'étape* on the far west side of the village. If staying in la Bastide, continue 2.4km west beyond Camps-sur-l'Agly along the route using the Stage 5a notes.

STAGE 5A

Camps-sur-l'Agly to Bugarach

Start	Camps-sur-l'Agly *gîte d'étape*
Finish	Bugarach village centre
Distance	11.5km
Ascent	580m
Descent	630m
Time	4hr
Refreshments	None until Bugarach, which has some small restaurants and a little farm shop

This is the shortest stage on the Cathar Way. It's also a strikingly wild one with a couple of stubborn climbs that yield some of the broadest panoramas of the entire walk, making it breathtaking in more ways than one.

It is a remote stretch of walking, the only settlement on this stage being la Bastide – a hamlet made up of mostly ruined and crumbling buildings. A fairly constant companion, however, is the soaring presence of the Pech de Bugarach – the highest peak of the Corbières – which rises over 1200m and gives this area a distinctly dramatic bass note.

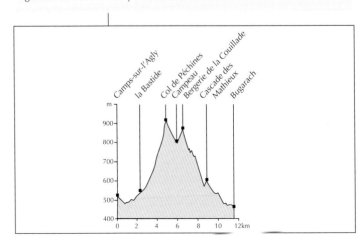

Beginning on the narrow road at the western end of **Camps-sur-l'Agly**, just beyond the *gîte d'étape*, set out on the track that goes off the lane to the northwest. At a fork shortly after, go right and gently descend to the River Agly. Cross the river over a small footbridge to the right and then rise up to meet a tarmac lane. Turn left along it.

Continue along the lane as it heads west out into the countryside and closer again to the buttressed eastern face of the Pech de Bugarach. The crumbling hamlet of la Bastide soon appears – the only settlement on today's route.

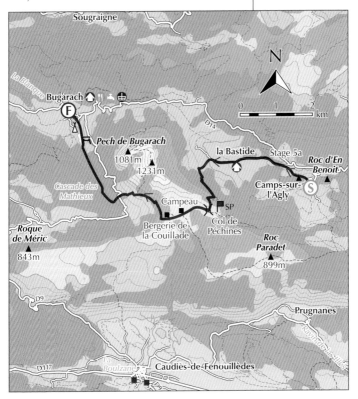

Route towards the Pech de Bugarach

The jagged limestone peak of the **Pech de Bugarach** rises to over 1230m and is hemmed in by similarly sharp needles and spurs of rock. Beneath it lie whole galleries of caves, many of which have never been explored.

Once through **la Bastide**, continue along the lane for another 600 metres before turning left onto a track. Now begins quite a long and steep climb. At another track meeting, turn left and climb into thickening woodland, zigzagging as the route ascends. At an area of open ground the path swings to the right into a patch of box and beech trees. On this last part of the climb the ascent becomes very steep, but this doesn't last too long.

Emerge onto an open ridge, with spectacular views over the landscape. You can pick out the Fenouillèdes hills to the south, with the mountains of the eastern Pyrenees beyond; the Pech de Bugarach nearby on the right; and the Corbières hills lying far to the east.

Descend the open slope on the other side of the ridge, going down through woodland to reach the **Col de Péchines** where a dwelling once stood, entirely digested by vegetation. At the signposted junction take the path to the right beside the low stone wall. Descending now, the path enters a basin of open land, thinly forested. At a fork, turn left.

At the bottom of the slope is the remote **Campeau** site – a sprawling complex of ruined farm buildings. There's also an artificial lake and an old well, all surrounded by pastureland. ▸

Just beyond the ruins of Campeau, pass the man-made lake to the left and the well to the right. Go up the slope straight ahead and follow the faint track to a steeply slanting open pastureland. Keep a keen eye out for waymarks as the path cuts right up the meadow to the top right-hand corner. It slips through the thicket of woodland bordering the top of the pasture and passes another ruin, **Bergerie de la Couillade** – a stone sheepfold also being slowly reclaimed by the natural world. ▸

At the wooden signpost, turn right uphill on a footpath which quickly arrives at a track. Turn left and reach a new hill summit, teetering at the top of a new valley. The views along the next section are sublime, sweeping across layers of hills and forest. Follow the track; it soon takes a sharp right and descends through beech trees. At the bottom of the slope, leave the track and head up the path bearing right through woodland, passing through an electric fence. ▸

At Campeau the north variant briefly aligns with Stage 5 of the main (south) route connecting Saint-Paul-de-Fenouillet to Caudiès-de-Fenouillèdes.

The south route diverges again here; to join it, turn left at the signpost and follow the instructions in Stage 5. It's around 7km down to Caudiès-de-Fenouillèdes.

The ruin of Bergerie de la Couillade

Once on more open ground, the huge Pech de Bugarach dominates on the right. Continue along the hillside, which has a pastoral feel to it, dotted with trees and still with magnificent open views alongside. Descend steadily for quite a while, passing a turning up to the right, signposted as the Sentier de Pech de Bugarach, which snakes up to the summit. Ignore it and continue instead to a fork and turn left, the path descending further to eventually meet the D45 road.

The way down is quite slippery and loose but only short, so it is worth checking out what is probably the best waterfall on the Cathar Way.

Cross the road and walk through a small gate to descend through woodland to a river. The path here can be slippery when wet. If the river is too high, go back up to the road and continue along it for 3.5km to reach Bugarach. Otherwise, cross the river and bear right through the woodland. After 500 metres you'll come to a little off-trail path signposted to the **Cascade des Mathieux**, a beautiful woodland waterfall. ◄

Continuing on the route, pass through more woodland and an impressive conical rocky peak, the path hugging the hillside above a narrow valley which plunges quickly out of view. A good 2km beyond the waterfall, the path crosses the same river again. Pass a lake to the left (with a **picnic bench**) to join a track that leads out to the D14. Continue along the road to head into **Bugarach**.

A 1000-year-old village with a 16th-century (or earlier) château, **Bugarach** lies directly beneath the 1230m Pech de Bugarach, whose shadow looms long. The village itself is said to be the place novelist Jules Verne holidayed, and where he was inspired by the desolate mountain landscape to write his science fiction novel *Journey to the Centre of the Earth* in 1864.

A traditional farming village, Bugarach does have a nascent tourism trade, with no fewer than three *chambres d'hôtes* and a campsite.

STAGE 6A

Bugarach to Quillan

Start	Bus stop, Bugarach village centre
Finish	Bridge over River Aude, Quillan
Distance	23.25km
Ascent	980m
Descent	1150m
Time	7hr
Refreshments	None until Quillan

This stage holds some of the most mysterious of Cathar locations, tucked away in deep folds of woodland and rock. Château des Templiers and Rennes-le-Château both have legends attached to them of treasure and conspiracy, Cathar or otherwise. Both can be glimpsed from the trail but are not directly passed.

As a day's walk it is not particularly difficult, but as usual there aren't really any places to find food. Thankfully, Quillan makes an excellent place to stay and refuel at the end of the stage.

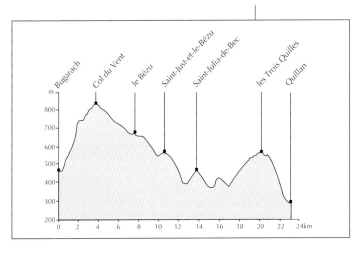

From the centre of **Bugarach**, by the old bus stop and old school building, walk along the road towards the rocky ridge of the Pech de Bugarach. Turn right down the lane signposted 'Maison de la Nature et de la Randonnée', cross the stream and bear left with the lane.

As the lane bears left again, take the footpath off to the right uphill, waymarked as the Cathar Way Nord.

The pretty village of Bugarach with the Pech in the background

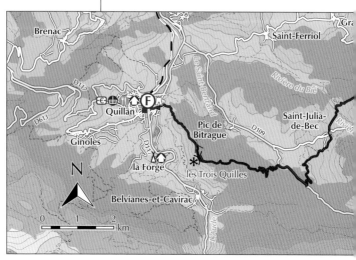

Follow this rocky and possibly muddy path up into open fields and then into the forest of Bugarach. After entering its fringes, continue climbing for 500 metres and turn a sharp left at a fork, pushing deeper into the pines. Further on into the forest, at another fork, turn a sharp right along a forestry track.

Follow this track for nearly 2km as it very gradually climbs further to the **Col du Vent**. ▶ The route continues to the right, over a cattle grid.

On a clear day, to the left and south, the Pyrenees are visible.

The next 4km are all downhill through the forest of Saint-Just-et-le-Bézu. Over to the right is the ridge where the Château des Templiers once stood, and to the north you can see as far as the Montagne Noire beyond Carcassonne.

CHÂTEAU DES TEMPLIERS

Also known as the Château du Bézu or Albedun, it seems this forgotten fortress had more to do with the Cathars than the Templars (the medieval order of Christian knights). Cathar bishops did apparently use the castle to hide from the French, but it surrendered in 1210 after the fall of Château de Termes.

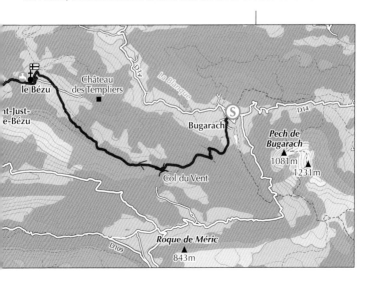

However, it's the Templar rumours that stick. It is thought that the castle's lord was connected somehow to the Templar Knights and that Templar treasure was kept here, smuggled out when under attack from the French in the 14th century. Ghost stories of a tolling bell and apparitions of spectral Templar knights surround the ruin today.

Just over halfway down you'll cross a cattle grid and come to a fork: stay straight (right) on the principal track downhill.

Pass over another cattle grid as you head out to open countryside, soon passing a farm building on the left. Join a tarmac lane and 400 metres further on turn left downhill. ◄ After 150 metres along the lane, fork right onto a track going uphill. Terrace the hillside for 600 metres, possibly glimpsing Rennes-le-Château which lies on a hilltop 5km to the northwest.

On reaching a **cemetery**, turn left as way-marked, down towards the hamlet of **le Bézu**. Pass the Romanesque church on the right and wind down into the hamlet through allotments. ◄

The lane swings left, passing a water trough, and then right. Join the tarmac D609 crossed earlier, and go right, passing stables. The road bears to the right past farmland and continues for just over 1km, with a little rise at the

On a clear day a solid lone tower of Puivert Castle can be seen, still over 20km away at the end of Stage 8.

This church in its current form dates to the 17th century, but it was first mentioned in the 11th century.

RENNES-LE-CHÂTEAU

This hilltop site has its own ancient treasure legend, this time involving a parish priest by the name of Bérenger Saunière. Arriving in Rennes-le-Château in 1885, he soon began making inexplicably lavish additions and renovations to his church, buying land and building his own villa. It was soon widely speculated he had unearthed some mysterious hidden Cathar or Gallic fortune perhaps left somewhere in the grounds many centuries before, maybe even by Cathars who had escaped Montségur during the siege of 1243–4. Whatever happened, Saunière took the secret of his fortune to his grave.

The story of hidden treasure, along with some mysterious symbols found installed in the church, has spawned all kinds of conspiracy theory progeny: connections with the Templars, old secret societies or the Holy Grail. And

Rennes-le-Château has lived on in popular culture: the name Saunière features in Dan Brown's blockbuster tale of religious intrigue and conspiracy *The Da Vinci Code*. The mystery attracts many people to the area to this day.

end to meet the D46. Turn left onto the D46, passing a stone cross on the right.

Follow the road for a short way, cross a bridge, and 100 metres later turn left off the road onto a footpath. The path turns into a track to emerge back onto the D46 and leads into the quaint hamlet of **Saint-Just-et-le-Bézu**, where there's an old school and church.

With the hamlet's *lavoir* (wash house) on the left, turn right onto a narrower lane going downhill. After passing a stone cross the lane soon stops and you fork onto the footpath off to the left, descending into sparse woodland.

The next hamlet, Saint-Julia-de-Bec, can be seen not too far ahead. Continue downhill towards it, emerging at a clearing on bare rock. At a fork here, take either way as they soon rejoin. Shortly after, cross an often-dry stream bed.

On reaching a tarmacked road go left, passing a former mill on the right. Climb the tarmac lane for 800 metres into **Saint-Julia-de-Bec**, a pretty hamlet with Occitan street signs. At a T-junction in the hamlet turn right. About 50 metres up the road, in the centre, pass a pretty fountain on the right and a rather grand bus shelter – a good place for a rest.

When ready to continue, instead of going straight on under an arched building as signposted to Quillan, go left up La Placetta and then right on La Font d'Amont. Follow this road to its end and discover said font, a sunken washplace. Continue straight on the grassy track as signposted.

After 200 metres you'll come to a tarmac road and a fork: turn right downhill. Keep left (straight on) when another tarmac road joins from the right. The lane bears to the right. Ignore other smaller turnings until a waymarked track goes off downhill to the left. Follow this track and cross over a stream by a solid bridge after 1km. Then begin a gradual climb of just under 1km to reach the **D109**.

Turn right on the road and follow it downhill for 1km. After crossing two bridges, turn left onto a jeep track. It immediately forks: go left on the lower track. You now begin another steady climb, this one lasting 3.5km, which at first zigzags up the hill and then eases to traverse the hillside westward.

On reaching a clearing, go straight on. The turning off to the left along the 'Sentier Panoramique' is a short diversion that affords excellent views from les Trois Quilles of the dramatic Aude basin, but staying on the Cathar Way offers a wonderful perspective back onto the three hamlets already passed through today.

At a junction of signposted tracks, take the first left for the Cathar Way, not the second. (The second summits the 647m Pic de Bitrague.) Quillan immediately comes into view, surprisingly close.

It's a narrow and enjoyable path heading gradually downhill, overlooking the Aude Valley, with a glimpse of the village of Ginoles (another village you'll go through later on the Cathar Way) extending westwards from Quillan.

At a bench at a staggered crossroads, go straight on downhill. A little further on, pass a random bit of fence installed on the path and go along the main track to the right. Ignore the two left turns. At another clearing shortly afterwards, take the track slightly to the right to eventually emerge on a tarmacked road in the relatively new housing

The view opens up beyond Quillan to Ginoles

estate on the outskirts of **Quillan**. Go straight on downhill for 70 metres, and as the road bends to the right, follow the lane off to the left with a 'No Through Road' sign.

This lane soon leads to the forbidding Quillan Castle. Continue downhill to come out onto the road on one side of the old bridge over the River Aude. Cross it to enter the centre of Quillan.

A bustling country town, **Quillan** is a popular base of tourists exploring Cathar country, as well as being a centre for rafting and river sports in the Aude gorges.

The imposing square-shaped Quillan Castle was the site of a fortress for Cathar opposition forces during the Albigensian Crusade, although what stands today is not the original castle. The town church was originally 14th-century but has since been almost wholly renovated.

In Quillan there are banks, grocery shops, a pharmacy, cafés and restaurants, and a market on Wednesday and Saturday mornings. The selection of accommodation is wide but there is a youth hostel in la Forge if preferred – around 1.5km out of town along the D117 road.

Quillan is the biggest town on the route and has a history dating back over a thousand years

STAGE 7A

Quillan to Puivert

Start	Bridge over River Aude, Quillan
Finish	Place de l'Église, Puivert village (Stage 7a ends at Coudons)
Distance	20km
Ascent	840m
Descent	650m
Time	6hr (or 7hr+ including visit to Puivert Castle)
Refreshments	None until Puivert
Public transport	Bus 402 to Carcassonne and 500 to Perpignan, with the latter stopping at Axat, Puilaurens, Caudiès-de-Fenouillèdes and Saint-Paul-de-Fenouillet, as well as bus 409 on to Puivert

The last stage of the north variant has lovely wide vistas of tousled and rocky countryside, but it is quite a strenuous one, particularly at the beginning where you do most of the day's ascending in a steep climb to Coudons. Here the north variant rejoins the main route and follows the last 13km of Stage 8. (The statistics listed here are for the stage in total so include that last stretch all the way to Puivert.)

From just over the bridge into **Quillan**, cross the Place de la République to the right and continue straight on along Rue de l'Église towards the church clock tower. Pass the church to the right and come to a tarmac road. Turn left at the main square and walk along Avenue Sauzède to the main road through Quillan, and at the T-junction turn right.

Come to a crossroads by a hotel and turn left on the D79 towards Ginoles. Cross the railway line and follow the road round to the left. ◄ The D79 soon bears off to the right, but carry on along a smaller road parallel to the train tracks. After 200 metres turn right onto Chemin du Castillou – a small lane leading to a little settlement of

An alternative horse-riding route is signposted to the right; this rejoins at Nébias.

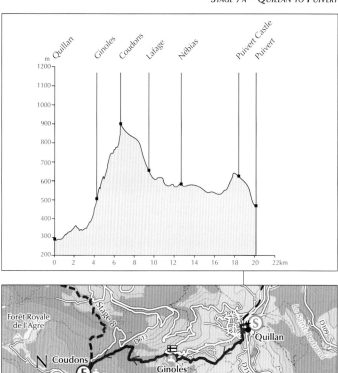

houses. The tarmac soon ends and the track winds away from the buildings to open pasture.

After a further 500 metres, fork to the right, coming to a T-junction where the track bends to the right, widens and heads towards Ginoles village. At the bottom of the hill, do not cross the stream but turn left onto a footpath and walk along the bank for 120 metres until you can cross over on a stone bridge. Walk towards the village, ignoring a small

Pass through the village of Ginoles to rejoin the main route

Ginoles is a small fortified village of Narbonne, with a population of only a few hundred.

There's drinking water here if you need it.

turning off to the left, to reach a T-junction where you turn left to continue in the general direction of the village.

Hit a tarmac lane and go left along it, passing allotments and dipping just below the village of **Ginoles**. After 200 metres you turn sharp right and cross a stream. Go steeply uphill on the tarmac into the village. ◄

Once at the top of this small hill, turn left up Rue Principale. Turn right at a covered seating area with a *lavoir*. ◄ Before reaching the D79, turn left and pass an impressive pine-framed cemetery. Walk up this lane, the Rue du Château d'Eau, for 200 metres to reach a gravel clearing and a metal cross.

Proceed uphill to the right, walking over black, crumbling rock. The next 1km is very well waymarked and the path zigzags gradually uphill. Eventually, at a fork of tracks, go left and pass through a red-and-white barrier.

Now climbing more steeply with no kindly zigzagging, the path bears at first to the right, affording huge open views of the Aude Valley, including Quillan and the Trois Quilles ridge. Then it swings left, traversing bare rock and soon enough arriving at a wide forest track. Turn right onto this and continue for 400 metres, and then just before a bend to the right, go left on a path up into the forest.

A further 1km uphill leads to **Coudons**. On reaching the D613 on the village outskirts, turn right. From here, pick up Stage 8 of the main route heading to Puivert.

PUIVERT TO FOIX

STAGE 9
Puivert to Espezel

Start	Place de l'Église, Puivert village
Finish	Place du Calcat, Espezel
Distance	16.75km
Ascent	650m
Descent	240m
Time	5hr
Refreshments	None until Espezel
Public transport	Bus 409 to Quillan from Puivert

There are no Cathar castles on this stage but there are remnants from a different period of violent history: World War II. This part of Languedoc was an important centre for the Maquis of the French Resistance and saw several bouts of fighting between Allied forces, the Resistance and German troops. A short way off today's trail lies the Poste de Commandement (PC) du Maquis, a reconstructed stone cabin that was the local Resistance HQ during the war.

The landscape changes somewhat as you wind your way between forestry land and wide pasture. Although pretty flat, the surrounding mountains give it a high, alpine feel that continues in the stages to come.

Leaving the centre of **Puivert**, cross the river and turn left towards La Buvette du Lac (snack hut) and the lakeside, as waymarked. Pass to the left of the hut and follow the tarmac lane which bridges over a stream and out into the countryside. The stocky tower of Puivert Castle stands on the left, and an airstrip over to the right is regularly used by gliders.

At a crossroads, turn right and then immediately right again onto a smaller track. Follow this track for over

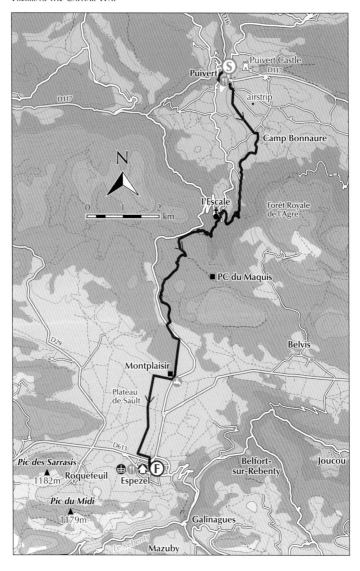

1km out into the flat open land, parallel to the airstrip. At another crossroads with farm buildings on the left, go straight on to begin a gentle climb up the track.

Only 100 metres up this track, fork right. Ignore the track soon after to the left leading up to the hamlet of **Camp Bonnaure**, passing instead below the hamlet. Again ignoring a farm track off to the left soon after, continue straight on.

The track descends, crosses a stream and bends to the right (ignore the two left turnings along it). Carry on winding along the valley flat, crossing another stream after 1km. Beyond this crossing, rise to join a tarmac lane and turn left along it. After 600 metres, shortly after passing an abandoned farmhouse on the right (dated 1837 on its façade), the tarmac lane stops at a turning point and the path continues straight into the woods ahead.

This woodland footpath begins to climb, bending to the left and then the right. At a junction in the woods, take the sharp right turning downhill, winding your way down through the trees for 500 metres to meet the stream once again. Ignore the path straight on, signposted 'Sentier Historique', and cross the narrow footbridge over the stream. Climb on an earth track for 400 metres to a tarmac lane in the hamlet of **l'Escale**.

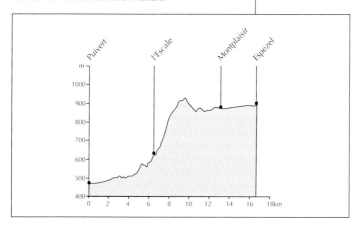

Turn left, and after 100 metres bear to the right with the lane as waymarked uphill. At the top, bear left and take the turning to the left of the Romanesque church along Rue du Maquis.

L'ESCALE

The village of l'Escale is known for its connection with the Maquis French Resistance fighters during World War II ('Maquis' is a broad term for guerrilla resistance, named after a thick, impenetrable underbrush commonly used as cover). L'Escale was eventually razed to the ground by German troops in August 1944 as reprisal. There is a commemorative plaque at the church.

Linked is the nearby PC du Maquis, a reconstructed stone cabin used by the French Resistance as a local headquarters. It too was destroyed in 1944, but not before all the fighters had escaped. Now rebuilt, it is open year-round.

Soon after the church, at a fork, turn right and leave l'Escale. Follow the principal track for 600 metres before forking off right on a rocky path that climbs into the forest. The path zigzags up the slope sensibly, but steeply in places, for 1km. At a path fork in the pine forest the route is waymarked right but either way is fine – in fact the left cuts a zigzag.

Soon reach a junction of tracks and turn left and then immediately right as waymarked. Climb a scree-lined path through a conifer plantation. After 400 metres take a sharp right, also as waymarked. ◀

Turning left at this junction leads to the nearby rebuilt PC du Maquis.

Come to a messy fork in a forestry clearing. The only tree currently standing in the clearing has a waymark for a fork; turn left and follow the faint path. Emerge on the bend of an established forestry track and turn left onto it, going slightly downhill. At a small clearing carry straight on as the track s-bends through the woods.

Follow this track for 400 metres until it bends to the right. Here, take the footpath off to the left. If there's forestry machinery blocking the footpath go around it to the right as you'll see other people have done.

Further on through the woods you'll reach another forestry track. Turn left here and continue for only 70

metres before turning off onto a footpath that steps down into the woods, waymarked to the right. Follow this path to come to another track and again turn left. Some 600 metres later come out of the woods and see the beginnings of the Plateau de Sault, and beyond it – excitingly – mountains.

The Plateau de Sault near Espezel is used mostly for arable farming, potatoes being the biggest crop

Turn right down to the road and cross over to follow the Cathar Way. Walk parallel to the D120 for 600 metres along a grassy path, and then turn away from it to the right as you reach the corner of a fenced field. Walk with the woods on the right and the pasture on the left for 1km until you see the buildings of **Montplaisir**. Thread your way towards them, but just before hitting the D120 road turn right along a very straight track. ▶

Montplaisir has a drinking-water tap right on the trail.

Walk along this exposed track and turn left after 500 metres for Espezel. (The route to Comus goes straight on here, so the next stage returns and continues from this point.) Follow the track for almost 2.5km, going straight over a track crossroads almost at the halfway point. Turn left at a first T-junction, and at the second turn right and go under the D613 through a small tunnel to emerge into the Place du Calcat in **Espezel**.

A small farming community, **Espezel** sits right on the Plateau de Sault, a pancake-flat area of land hedged in by Pyrenean foothills. There is a small museum here detailing local life from the past century and exhibiting a variety of everyday objects, including an oil lamp very similar to one discovered at the 13th century village of Montségur.

Espezel has a hotel, a bar and a grocery shop.

The rural village of Espezel on the Plateau de Sault

STAGE 10

Espezel to Comus

Start	Place du Calcat, Espezel
Finish	Comus village centre
Distance	20km
Ascent	730m
Descent	440m
Time	6hr
Refreshments	None until Comus

This stage traverses some of the most dazzling landscapes on the Cathar Way, crossing mountain plateaux, gullies and gorges and reaching the highest point of the trail, just before the Col de la Gargante, at an altitude of 1356m. It also passes above the cleft of the dramatic Frau Gorge on its way to the village of Comus, enfolded in the mountains.

While there aren't any Cathar castles on this stage, from the highpoint of the Plateau de Languerail the great fortress of Montségur is sighted for the first time, still off in the distance perched romantically on its limestone *pog*.

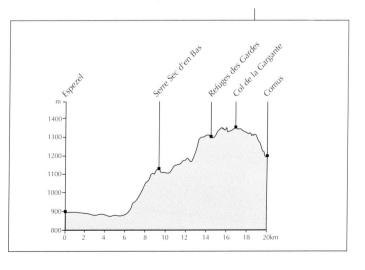

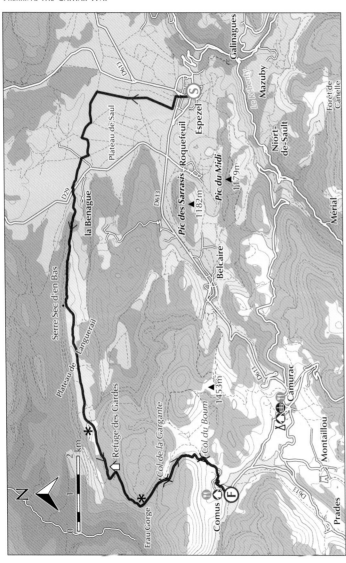

Retrace your footsteps from yesterday by heading out of **Espezel**, passing the little shop and going back under the road through the small tunnel. Turn left at the first track, and then follow the track to the right after nearly 400 metres. Walk across the bone-flat plateau for 2.2km, still retracing steps, to arrive back at the T-junction. Turn left at the signpost to Comus, and enter new territory.

Begin by following this still very flat track for just under 1km. When a track joins from the left, continue to the right. Some 500 metres later, at a fork, go left, and then ignore a grassy track off to the left soon after. Follow the route round to the right.

At a T-junction, turn right. After a further 200 metres, cross straight over the tarmacked D193 road to pick up the footpath alongside a fence. Follow the fence for nearly 1km, and when close to the D29 veer away from the fence and spot the route up a track across the road to the right. ▶

The hamlet of la Benague is tucked into a little valley over to the left.

This is where the climb begins, lasting for just over 2km and ascending about 200m. It starts fairly steeply but soon levels out, following the ridgeline up a rocky but shaded track to an upland plateau at an altitude of 1100m. Keep left as waymarked at any fork on the way up.

Shortly after the path levels out, emerge from the woods to a fence bordering an open meadow with expansive views of forested hills and mountains. Follow the footpath along the fence to the right. Soon after, go through a metal gate with a 'Prairies de Pâturage' sign. ▶

These high pastures are grazed by sheep and cows in the summer which often have the Pyrenean mountain dogs to protect them, so be aware.

Once on the open grassland, descend a little and pass to the left of the **Serre Sec d'en Bas ruin**. Follow the faint track across the meadow, bearing right and descending to pass through a small gate at the corner of the pasture. Beyond the gate, follow the line of beech trees, climbing past a thicket of blackthorn bushes. After 500 metres you'll arrive at another line of very large beech trees to lead you properly onto the **Plateau de Languerail**.

The highest plateau on the trail, **Plateau de Languerail** affords stunning views of Languedoc hill country and the first clear view of Montségur Castle, perched in the distance on a fairy-tale pinnacle.

*Over 1300m above
sea level on the
remote Plateau
de Languerail*

On a clear day you can also see the eastern Pyrenees, the fellow high plateau of Montagne de la Frau and the distant Montagne Noire region that rises from the plains of Toulouse.

Walk to the right of the beech trees and after 1km come to a T-junction. Turn right and follow a track round to the left with waymark posts at spaced-out points, climbing all the time. This is quite a slog but it's really the last bit of noticeable ascent of this stage, and offers the highest, broadest mountain views of the whole trail to distract you.

After the track flattens out, keep an eye out for an even better view of Montségur Castle. Carry on and after 500 metres come to a fork (not waymarked) of two significant tracks leading into the forest. Take the left option and wind through the trees for 1km to arrive at a clearing and a small hut – the **Refuge des Gardes** – which is unlocked.

*This track is the
highest point on
the Cathar Way,
at 1356m.*

Turn right here on the wide forest track leading gently uphill. It swings to the left and you walk along an established and attractively winding track with views across the Frau Gorge and with Montségur Castle still visible off to the right. ◀

After descending a little you'll soon come to the **viewpoint** of Pas de l'Ours, from which you can peer hundreds of metres down into the Frau Gorge. Walk on for 800 metres to reach the **Col de la Gargante**. At the junction of tracks at the col, go off to the right on the main track as waymarked.

As the descent to Comus begins, the track becomes tarmac and skirts the western side of a large grassy bowl called the Pla du Boum. Cross over another col – **Col du Boum** – and descend more steeply for 300 metres with an entirely new valley suddenly visible left and right. Keep a lookout for the old Cathar village of Montaillou, far over on the left. Take the footpath off to the right following the line of the fence, leading directly towards the village of Comus.

Frau Gorge from near the highest point on the Cathar Way

Montaillou village and castle held true to Cathar beliefs long after the fall of Montségur in 1244 – enough to merit the attention of the Inquisition sent to the Languedoc in the early 14th century to quash any remaining Cathar feeling. The subsequent records from the Inquisition capture minute detail of many aspects of rural medieval life in the village, and were used centuries later in the work *Montaillou* by French historian Emmanuel Le Roy Ladurie.

Cross over a tarmac lane and continue downhill on the footpath. It zigzags steeply downhill and the path soon becomes a tarmac lane. Enter the village, following the waymarks to the left to arrive at the old school building on the right in the centre of **Comus**.

COMUS

A mountain village in the alpine style, Comus is surrounded by pine forest and limestone mountains where even in summer the jagged Pic de Soularac (2368m) is often still snow-capped. This small outdoorsy community hosts skiers in winter, and is also popular with cavers: the limestone around Comus is riddled with over 200 caves.

There are a number of accommodation options in Comus, including the well-established *gîte d'étape*. Alternatively, continue on to Camurac 3km further along the D20, which also has a *gîte* and campsite, as well as a shop and café.

STAGE 11

Comus to Montségur

Start	Comus village centre
Finish	Main street, Montségur village
Distance	14km
Ascent	700m
Descent	950m
Time	5hr (or 6½hr including visit to Montségur Castle)
Refreshments	None until Montségur village

A short stage which ends at the base of Montségur Castle – the most famous of all the Cathar castles and probably the historical highlight of the whole trail. Although it's technically the next day's stage that goes directly past the castle, there should be enough time after this walk to visit the castle in the afternoon.

Accommodation is available but limited in Montségur village, so there is the option of continuing on the trail to neighbouring Montferrier 4km further on (see Stage 12).

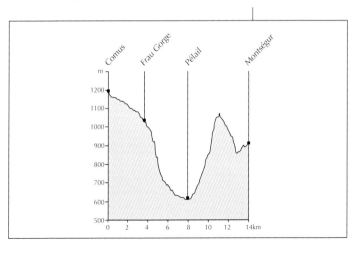

From the centre of **Comus**, follow the waymarks downhill to a restaurant/bar at a track junction. Turn right onto a small lane and head towards the Frau Gorge. This lane soon becomes a gravel track as it heads into darker, thicker forest hemmed in by high-sided cliffs.

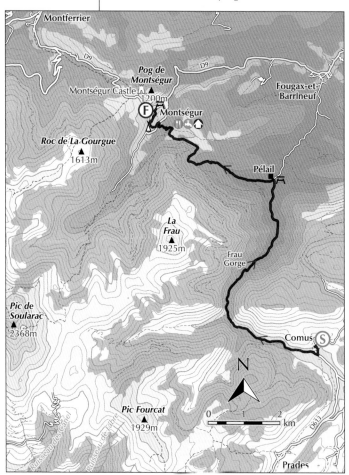

After 1km, at a fork, take the right on the flat track instead of the uphill option, and head further towards the gorge. After a further 2km, where the track bends to the left uphill, take the footpath that goes straight on into the **Frau Gorge**.

The route descends over 400m through the Frau Gorge

> Carved out by the River Hers as it makes its way from the mountains above Ax-les-Thermes to the River Ariège just south of Toulouse, the **Frau Gorge** is a fantastically deep and narrow cleft hewn out of the local limestone. The Cathar Way winds along the valley bottom for 2km and over that distance drops more than 400m.

Follow this rocky footpath downhill along the dark and cool gorge bottom for 2km, enclosed all the while by the sheer-sided rock, until fairly abruptly you come out to a tarmac road, the D5. Follow it as it now gently descends for a further 2.5km to reach a **picnic area** on the right and a road turning on the left. Go left as signposted towards Pélail.

Pass through the attractive little farm complex that is the sum total of **Pélail**, after which the tarmac lane turns to an earthen track. Now begins a long ascent, which isn't too bad for the first 1.5km as it follows a babbling stream to the left. But after crossing the stream the ascent steepens considerably for around 1km, without much zigzagging to help. Fortunately, it's through shady woodland on springy forest floor.

Over halfway up this steep section, turn right up a more established track and climb steps to reach a bend in the path to the right. Here it finally flattens out at over 1000m elevation. Having recovered from the climb, follow this wonderfully easy path round the hill. The trees thin out and you soon get another glimpse of Montségur Castle.

Plunge back into woodland and descend towards the castle. The decline eases as it follows the perimeter of pastureland, and soon afterwards comes to a tarmac road. Turn left here and continue downhill, but only for 50 metres until the road bends to the left, where you take the footpath off to the right.

Zigzag down through the trees, turning right as waymarked at a small earthen junction. Skirting a very alpine-looking field to the left, admire a great view of the ridged Pic de Soularac (2368m) at the end of the valley.

Across the valley to Montségur Castle and village

Ignore a right turn signposted to the Tour du Roc de la Mousse and continue towards a bridge crossing a stream. Follow the gravel track up to the right from the bridge, and at the top of a small rise turn left onto the **D9**.

In due course, come to a couple of grassy turnings off to the right, taking the second one and following it as it gently ascends round to the right. It leads between smallholding plots and emerges into a car park: continue to the far end.

Pick up the D9 road once more, but only for 20 metres before taking a waymarked footpath down to the right leading to picnic benches. Turn left before the benches and walk along a stone wall and through more peaceful garden allotments. The path eventually winds up to the road in **Montségur village**.

Turn right and come to a restaurant on the right. The Cathar Way (Stage 12) continues uphill directly opposite the restaurant. If you want to visit Montségur Castle, follow the beginning of the next stage's instructions to get to the footpath leading up to it.

A pretty village bordered by vegetable allotments and popular with holidaymakers, **Montségur** has a small tourist information office, a couple of café-restaurants and a few places to stay – although no shop.

The village also has a one-room archaeological museum exhibiting a number of artefacts from the Cathar period, including coins and weaponry. The admission ticket for Montségur Castle also permits entry to the museum, which is open March–October.

MONTSÉGUR CASTLE

Clinging precariously to the top of a humped limestone *pog*, Montségur Castle is popularly known as the last redoubt of the Cathars. Originally built in the eighth century, it was refortified by southern nobleman Raymond de Péreille in 1204 and used by the Cathars, led by Guilhabert de Castres over the crusade years. In that time, hundreds of Cathar men and women, along with some homeless *faidits* (displaced southern knights), sought refuge within Montségur's walls, and it soon became the seat of the Cathar church.

Montségur Castle sits atop its pog 1200m above sea level

Initially the Host did not apparently set its sights on capturing Montségur. But when in 1242 a group of warriors from the castle set out and slaughtered Inquisition officials at Avignonet, the response was swift: the attack on Montségur began in the spring of 1243.

The siege dragged on for many months, the castle's position making it seemingly unassailable. But an act of astonishing daring saw a group of French soldiers scale the sheer rock under the cover of darkness and capture a lookout post, tipping the balance in the crusaders' favour.

Commander Pierre-Roger de Mirepoix surrendered in early 1244. The Cathars were ordered to renounce their faith or die: 225 chose the latter and were burned at the stake at the base of the hill. This grim place is called the Prat dels Cremats (Field of the Burned) and is marked today with a stone cross.

Montségur has long been considered the secret location of the legendary Cathar treasure, smuggled out shortly before the surrender. It was rumoured this treasure was some mystical or magical relic, or even the Holy Grail itself. The story continues in popular culture, most recently in Kate Mosse's historical mystery novel *Labyrinth*, which features the lost Cathar treasure and a fictionalised account of the crusade and the siege of Montségur.

Today the castle's skeletal remains are mostly dated from its later life as a garrison for the French. It is open all year except January, and involves a stiff but rewarding climb up the *pog* to its entrance. Although the remains are scant, the view from the top is quite something: the arc of the Pyrenees, Roquefixade Castle ahead on the trail (Stage 12), and even the outer fringes of Toulouse are visible on a clear day.

STAGE 12

Montségur to Roquefixade

Start	Main street, Montségur village
Finish	Roquefixade *gîte d'étape*
Distance	16.5km (or 17.75km including visit to Montségur Castle)
Ascent	690m (or 840m including visit to castle)
Descent	840m (or 990m including visit to castle)
Time	5hr (or 6½hr if visiting Montségur Castle)
Refreshments	Supermarket at Villeneuve-d'Olmes 4km off route along the D9 northeast of Montferrier; restaurant Les Sapins shortly after is actually on the route. A cheery café-bar in the *gîte d'étape* in Roquefixade.
Public transport	Bus 450 from Montségur to Lavelanet and bus 451 on to Foix

Bookended by two beautiful Cathar castles – Montségur and Roquefixade – the penultimate stage of the Cathar Way is a picturesque and rewarding walk through woodland and along the valley side with some incredible views of the Ariège mountains and the castles. There are even a couple of possibilities to stop and pick up refreshments – a rarity on the Cathar Way.

In **Montségur**, walk up the main road, opposite the restaurant, quickly arriving in front of the church. ▶ Walk up to the left of the toilet block and round to the right to pass the *mairie*. Then, at a T-junction, walk to the left and slightly uphill to the bend of the D9. Go right here, passing the cemetery on the right.

There are public toilets and a drinking-water tap here.

After 100 metres, at another road bend, leave the D9 and take the narrow lane uphill to the left. Follow this lane for 500 metres as it gently rises and curves to the right, between open pastures, yielding a new view of Montségur Castle. On meet the D9 again, cross over onto the footpath which soon becomes a sunken lane for a short time before meeting the entrance path up to the castle, cutting across a grassy field. ▶

This area is the Prat dels Cremats (Field of the Burned) – the place where 225 Cathars were put to death after the siege of Montségur in 1244.

Carry straight on, skirting the field. (If returning from the castle, turn right with the castle behind.) Then fork left a short way afterwards. This narrow path terraces round a hillside and then descends to join the **D9**.

Turn right on the road and follow it as it bends to the left. After a short while, a little wooden gate appears down to the left, with several red-and-white crosses painted all over it. Formerly the Cathar Way, this small section has been rerouted along the road – a longer and rather pointless diversion, requested by the landowner. If the gate has again been repainted with red-and-white stripe waymarks, then proceed through the gate, following the track down to the stream.

Otherwise, follow the road downhill for 900 metres, passing a house and then reaching a cluster of buildings on the left, where the waymarked diversion turns sharp left into the valley. Follow a path – sometimes inexplicably uphill – towards a junction of paths. Turn right down the valley besides the stream. (The old route rejoins at this point from the left.)

Potter along by the stream in the woods, crossing it several times. After 1km, cross the D909 and continue straight along the footpath. Cross the stream again over a

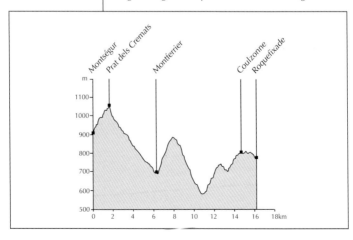

wooden footbridge, after which another path joins from the left, down from the hamlet of Céries.

Continue down the valley along the bank, passing a hamlet and a farmhouse on the right before joining a tarmac lane on the outskirts of Montferrier. Carry straight on along the lane, ignoring side turnings. The tarmac disappears briefly and reappears as you pass by a bridge. Then, after passing a campsite on the right, cross the main road bridge over the River Touyre into **Montferrier**. ▶

Soon after the bridge, turn sharp left uphill. After 100 metres fork right onto a lane. Climb out of town for 200 metres, ignoring any side turnings, until a grassy path

Montferrier no longer has a shop, but if there's a real need you can continue 2km down the road off route to Villeneuve-d'Olmes which has a supermarket.

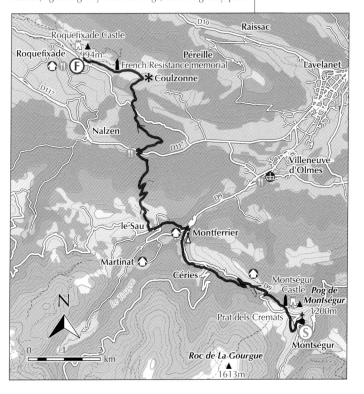

131

leaves the lane at a bend. Follow this path; the grass soon turns to cobble and leads up into light woodland.

In due course the path flattens out a little. At a fork with a metal cross, go straight on to the left, and 40 metres further on at another fork, go right. Cross a tarmacked lane and continue to climb the hill, crossing another road – the D209 – four more times. The trail then actually joins the D209, continuing straight along it for 70 metres before turning right into the hamlet of **le Sau**.

Walk through the tiny settlement and continue along the lane, which soon becomes a track and skirts the hillside for 700 metres. ◄ On reaching a wooden gate, go through it and begin a descent of over 2.5km. The path zigzags gradually down the hillside and affords the first clear look of Roquefixade and its castle. At the valley bottom, follow a stream and pass a stone building with a large water trough.

There are good views down the valley and over to Montségur Castle on the right.

On reaching a surfaced lane the route continues to the right, leading up to the **D117**. ◄ Up at the road, turn left and walk along it for 150 metres before carefully crossing it and heading into woodland on a footpath. Climb gradually for nearly 1km and reach a fork; turn left and climb for only a little longer. The path flattens out and winds through woodland for 1.5km to meet a minor road – the D9a.

Alternatively, 100 metres to the left is restaurant Les Sapins – open Wednesday–Sunday.

Cross the road and follow the tarmac lane opposite uphill for 1km to reach the charming hamlet of **Coulzonne**. A kind of fairy-tale landscape unfolds from here, with Montségur Castle on its own little hill to the east, and snowy mountains and verdant foothills stretching to the west.

Views of the Pyrenees from the hamlet of Coulzonne

Walk through Coulzonne, bearing left to follow a track slightly uphill. Ignore a couple of parallel tracks going

Roquefixade rooftops with Montségur Castle now far behind

off to the right and follow the main waymarked track for 800 metres. The trail passes a **French Resistance memorial** and continues round to the left. ▶

The track terraces along the hillside for 1km to reach the eastern edge of **Roquefixade**, the castle and mountains rising ever closer. Ignore a fork to the right by a road sign and carry on straight to the left and down into the village. On reaching the houses, keep straight on and reach a junction with *gîte* signposts, following whichever you decide to stay at. (Turn right uphill for the largest *gîte d'étape*.)

A rectilinear village developed after the Cathar period, **Roquefixade** has two *gîtes d'étape*, both centrally situated. The main one has a café-bar attached which opens in the afternoon.

A conical monument stands here to commemorate almost 20 local people who died during a German attack shortly before the liberation on 6 July 1944.

ROQUEFIXADE CASTLE

A castle built to watch the road leading from Mirepoix to Foix, Roquefixade was argued over periodically by the counts of Toulouse and the counts of Foix. After the crusade the castle passed to the French Crown and used as a garrison.

In the early 17th century the Crown ordered the castle to be completely destroyed, with the crumbling ruin now the only remnant.

The castle is free to visit but beware of the vertiginous drops and high winds up on its lonely perch.

STAGE 13
Roquefixade to Foix

Start	Roquefixade *gîte d'étape*
Finish	Bridge over the Ariège River, Foix
Distance	20.25km (or 21km including visit to Roquefixade Castle)
Ascent	680m (or 745m including visit to castle)
Descent	1060m (or 1125m including visit to castle)
Time	6hr (or 7hr including visit to Roquefixade Castle)
Refreshments	None until the main road into Foix
Public transport	Train connection from Foix station to Toulouse with connections onto Carcassonne and Narbonne, as well as one direct train per day to Paris

A magnificent (for the most part) final stage of the Cathar Way, terracing along the Ariège Valley with sublime views of the Pyrenees and of all three nearby Cathar castles: Montségur, Roquefixade and Foix.

Unfortunately, the final stretch down into Foix has been somewhat tampered with. Previously a direct 4km, it is now a circuitous 7km and involves following the long and rather uninspiring main road into the city, which sadly does away with the chance of an elevated aspect of Foix Castle. You may choose to catch a bus for the last section; both options are detailed here.

Looking back towards Roquefixade, the castle rears up in the foreground with its village hanging above the rolling hills and the distant Montségur Castle almost lost to the horizon.

From the main *gîte d'étape* in **Roquefixade**, take the grassy track leading west from just outside its door. The track rises slightly to meet a cross monument at a T-junction: turn right and walk uphill towards and then beneath the craggy perch of Roquefixade Castle. Pass an information panel from where it's possible to see the ridge of the Tabe Massif, with both the Pic de Saint-Barthélemy (2348m) and the Pic de Soularac (2368m) along it.

Continue uphill, passing the turning off to the right up to Roquefixade Castle, signposted to the 'Château'. Continue straight on for 200 metres to a path fork, then go left downhill. ◄ Soon after, come to another fork and

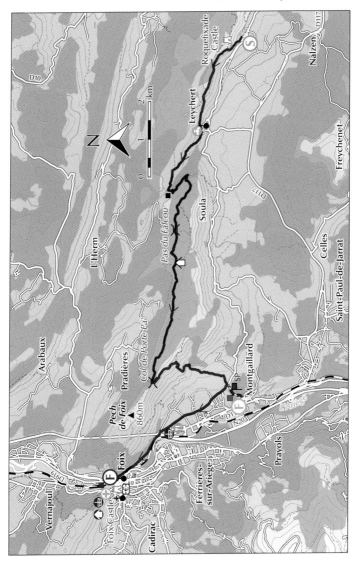

135

Leaving Roquefixade and walking below the remains of its castle high on its spur of rock

again go left. The path narrows and terraces along the hillside, still with amazing views. At a little clearing with a fork, go left and begin descending, forking left yet again 80 metres later onto a smaller path.

Nearly 1km on, at a junction of paths, turn left and follow the waymarks downhill to **Leychert**. On the outskirts of the village, pass a shrine with an iron cross. ◀ To continue, turn right onto the lane, and turn right uphill at a stone barn.

There is a drinking-water tap in Leychert, to the left at the church.

This is a steady climb for 1.4km, after which the trail flattens out and meets a junction of several tracks. Go left here as waymarked, and in a little break from climbing, the route begins to descend, undulating as it goes.

After 500 metres turn left, continuing downhill, and then follow the track as it swings uphill right, then left. Pass an old stone farmhouse and then a more modern farm complex. Continue straight on for a few hundred metres, passing a forest road off to the right to take a foot-path into the woods immediately afterwards.

It's a steep climb through the forest for just under 1km, but the route then flattens out for 200 metres before meeting a path fork. Go right here, following the red-and-white waymark. ◀ Shortly after, turn left onto a forestry track, passing through a single-bar barrier into deeper woodland.

The left turning is a local walking route marked with a red-and-yellow waymark.

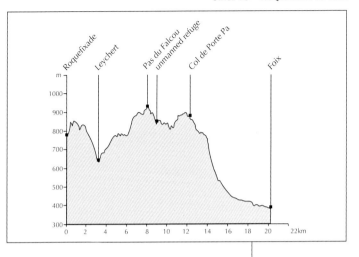

The track swings to the right and climbs steadily for 700 metres through beech forest. At a slight clearing at the **Pas du Falcou** there's a minor snag: the signpost for Foix points to the left, going off the forestry track, but a short way down this route there's a blockade, so we recommend ignoring this left turn and carrying on instead along the forestry track. Continue down, and after a further 1.1km, at a tight right bend, the Cathar Way rejoins from the left.

Continue on the forestry track, soon passing an unlocked **refuge** on the left. Ignore a turning off to the right 200 metres later, staying on the track for a further 1.6km as it climbs steadily and reaches a clearing with a track fork. Go right downhill and follow this track for 800 metres.

At the **Col de Porte Pa** there's a second snag: the path lies straight ahead but there's another blockade closing the route. A diversion notice has been placed on the fencing, and the re-route to Foix now goes off to the left. (If there is no diversion, go straight ahead, following the waymarks to pass by the **Pech de Foix** and descend the 4km into Foix.)

However, to follow the new route, go left from the barricade and follow the hillside gradually downhill for 1km. Then turn right off the principal track onto a narrow footpath that immediately descends very steeply, zigzagging sharply. After passing a stone ruin on the right, come out to a clearing marked with a cairn. Go left from the cairn and continue descending on a narrow path, following a yellow waymark on this descent.

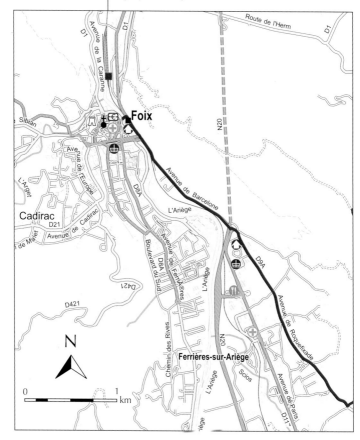

After passing through a metal gate the path flattens out, emerging from the trees to follow a stone wall, heading towards the Pyrenees. At a staggered crossroads, just after crossing a stream, turn right to continue downhill. Join an access track and follow it downhill to the left. The track comes out at the D9a on the outskirts of the village of Montgaillard, only a few kilometres outside of Foix.

Another diversion notice has been placed at this junction, recommending walkers take the bus the remaining distance to Foix, and providing a bus route timetable from the nearby *mairie* (town hall) to the city centre. To do this, go straight over the D9a and walk down the tarmac lane for 700 metres. Cross over the next road, pass by a car park and a primary school on the left, and continue along Rue du Pic which leads to the main road in **Montgaillard**. The *mairie* is on the left, and you'll find the bus stop nearby.

If you would prefer to walk into Foix, turn right along the D9a at the diversion's bus notice and keep going along this quiet road for 2.5km until you meet a busy roundabout. Go straight over, then go under the bridge and walk along the pavement by the road for a further 1.5km. Cross the first river bridge into **Foix**, thus completing the Cathar Way the old-fashioned way.

The terminus of the Cathar Way, **Foix** is one of the largest towns on the route, nestled along the Ariège River and crowned by its handsome castle. The medieval streets of its centre are narrow and winding and studded with buildings dating as far back as the 14th century. The large Saint-Volusien Church is at least 12th century, although it has since been pretty much wholly rebuilt.

Foix has all the major amenities including supermarkets, restaurants, hotels and banks. The railway station has direct onward connections to Toulouse and Narbonne, and from Foix it's also possible to travel into Andorra or Spain.

Foix: the final stop on the Cathar Way

FOIX CASTLE

Perched on a bold rocky outcrop at the convergence of the Ariège and Arget rivers and surrounded by the city, the castle had an important strategic position and belonged to the powerful Count of Foix. In the time of the crusade, Raymond-Roger de Foix was a Cathar sympathiser, whose own family were ordained Perfects, and a stout opponent of the crusaders.

Although attacked several times, Foix Castle was never captured, but it was forced to surrender in 1215 and given to the crusade leader Simon de Montfort. In 1218, the same year de Montfort was killed, the castle was recovered by the Foix family, but by 1229 Raymond-Roger's son Roger-Bernard was forced to submit finally to the Crown. The castle survived and was later used as a prison.

Foix Castle, still intact today, has had its two square towers since the 13th century (a seal from the time shows as much), while the round tower was added sometime before the 15th century. The castle is open all year and houses the Museum of the Province of Ariège, which is occupied mostly with archaeology and military history.

Looking towards the snow-capped Pyrenees (Stage 13)

APPENDIX A

Villages and towns with amenities

Note: only places directly on the Cathar Way are listed below.

Stage	Town/Village	Food shop(s)	Café/ Restaurant	Bank/ATM	Pharmacy
1	Port-la-Nouvelle	X	X	X	X
	Roquefort-des-Corbières	X	X		
	Durban-Corbières	X	X	X	
2	Tuchan	X	X	X	X
3	Padern		X		
	Quéribus Castle		X		
	Cucugnan	X	X		
4	Duilhac-sous-Peyrepertuse	X	X		
	Galamus Gorge		X		
	Saint-Paul-de-Fenouillet	X	X	X	X
5	Caudiès-de-Fenouillèdes	X	X		X
6	Puilaurens Castle		X		
	Axat	X	X	X	X
7	none				
8	Puivert		X		
4a	Duilhac-sous-Peyrepertuse		X		
	Cubières-sur-Cinoble		X		
5a	Bugarach		X		
6a	Quillan	X	X	X	X
7a	Puivert		X		
9	Espezel	X	X		
10	Comus		X		
11	Montségur		X		
12	Roquefixade		X		
13	Montgaillard	X	X		
	Foix	X	X	X	X

APPENDIX B

Accommodation

The following is a selection of places to stay for each of the stages of the Cathar Way. It is not an exhaustive list, but it covers various types of accommodation in each place, including: hotels, *chambres d'hôtes* (CH), B&Bs, *gîtes d'étape*, *auberges* and campsites.

Most of these can either be booked directly or through accommodation booking sites online. For *gîtes d'étape*, check: www.gites-de-france.fr

An asterisk * denotes author recommendation.

Main route

Arrival

Port-La-Nouvelle

Hôtel Restaurant Mediterranée
238 Bd du Front de Mer
11210 Port-la-Nouvelle
tel +33 4 68 48 03 08
www.logishotels.com

Port La Nouvelle Résidence
52 Rue Arago
11210 Port-la-Nouvelle
tel +33 6 29 32 50 06

Camping Municipal du Golf
406 Boulevard Francis Vals
11210 Port-la-Nouvelle
tel +33 4 68 48 00 98

Stage 1: Port-La-Nouvelle to Durban-Corbières

Along the way

*Domaine Castelsec B&B
Route de Fraïsse
11540 Roquefort-des-Corbieres
tel +33 6 33 20 19 96
castelsec11@gmail.com
www.domainecastelsec.fr

Durban-Corbières

*Chez Lola CH
3 Rue de l'égalité
11360 Durban-Corbières
tel +33 6 85 80 00 38

Sous l'abricotier CH
6 Rue du Presbytère
11360 Durban-Corbières
tel +33 6 16 74 28 71

Camping Municipal L'Espazo
11 Avenue du Bord de Berre
11360 Durban-Corbières
tel +33 4 68 45 06 81
(open mid June to mid September)

Stage 2: Durban-Corbières to Tuchan

Tuchan

*Le Couvent B&B
4 Rue du Bagnadou
11350 Tuchan
tel +33 6 51 16 65 57
samwebb12@me.com

Gîte Saint Roch
Planal de St Roch
11350 Tuchan
tel +33 6 77 61 30 52
gitesaintroch.tuchan@gmail.com
www.gitesaintroch.fr

Camping Le Relais d'Aguilar
16 Rue du Camping
11350 Tuchan
+33 (0)468454784
lerelaisdaguilar@gmail.com
www.relais-aguilar.com

Stage 3: Tuchan to Cucugnan

Padern

Gîte d'étape de Padern
3 Rue de l'Affenage
11350 Padern
tel +33 4 68 33 19 31

Cucugnan

Logis Hôtel La Table du Curé
25 Rue Alphonse Daudet
11350 Cucugnan
tel +33 9 70 35 53 96
www.auberge-la-table-du-cure.com

Auberge du Vigneron
2 Rue Achille Mir
11350 Cucugnan
tel +33 4 68 45 03 00
contact@auberge-vigneron.com
www.auberge-vigneron.com

Duilhac-sous-Peyrepertuse
(4km into Stage 4)

Hôtel L'hôstellerie du Vieux Moulin
24 Rue de la Fontaine
11350 Duilhac-sous-Peyrepertuse
tel +33 4 68 45 03 00
contact@auberge-vigneron.com
www.hostellerie-du-vieux-moulin.com

Gîte d'étape Communal
8 Chemin du Fort
11350 Duilhac-sous-Peyrepertuse
tel +33 6 74 04 93 76

Gîte d'étape Cathare
1 Rue des Genêts
11350 Duilhac-sous-Peyrepertuse
tel +33 4 68 48 45 73

**Stage 4: Cucugnan to
Saint-Paul-de-Fenouillet**

Saint-Paul-de-Fenouillet

*Domaine de Coussères CH
66220 Saint-Paul-de-Fenouillet
tel +33 4 68 59 23 55
www.cousseres.fr

Maison d'hôtes Le Galamus B&B
13 Rue de l'Aude
66220 Saint-Paul-de-Fenouillet

Camping de l'Agly
Avenue du 16 Août 1944
66220 Saint-Paul-de-Fenouillet
tel +33 4 68 59 09 09

**Stage 5: Saint-Paul-de-Fenouillet to
Caudiès-de-Fenouillèdes**

Prugnanes

Gîte d'étape Benjamin
4 Rue de Palmières
66220 Prugnanes
tel +33 4 68 50 03 14
www.gitebenjamin66.wixsite.com/
gitebenjamin66

Caudiès-de-Fenouillèdes

Hotel Relais de Laval
33 Avenue de Roussillon
66220 Caudiès-de-Fenouillèdes
tel +33 7 85 16 34 71
relaisdelaval@gmail.com
www.relaisdelaval.fr

Camping Municipal
Mairie Place de la Mairie
tel +33 4 68 59 92 64
www.mairie-caudies-fenouilledes.fr

Stage 6: Caudiès-de-Fenouillèdes to Axat

Puilaurens

Gîte d'étape
(3km east of Puilaurens, on the trail)
Hameau d'Aygues Bonnes
tel +33 4 68 20 51 90
colette.chazalet@wanadoo.fr

Chambres d'Hôtes La Folie
Route de la Boulzane
11140 Puilaurens
tel +33 4 68 69 19 85
info@lafolie.biz
www.lafolie.biz

Along the way

Gîte d'étape and Camping La Crémade
(2km northeast of Axat, on the trail)
Route de Perpignan
11140 Axat
tel +33 6 70 07 43 21

Axat

*Hotel Axat
101 Rte. Départementale
11140 Axat
tel +33 6 42 30 87 87
info@hotelaxat.comwww.hotelaxat.com

Camping Le Moulin du Pont d'Alies
Pont d'aliès
11140 Axat
tel +33 4 68 20 53 27
www.alies.fr

Stage 7: Axat to Quirbajou

Along the way

Chambres D'Hôtes Les Terrasses de Cailla
Impasse du Forgeron
11140 Cailla
tel +33 4 68 20 59 50

Gîte de Labeau – *gîte d'étape* in Labeau, 3km west of Marsa
11140 Marsa
tel +33 4 68 20 54 12

Quirbajou

*Gîte d'étape La Maison Jaune
8 Rue du Dépiquage
11500 Quirbajou
tel +33 4 68 20 18 86

Stage 8: Quirbajou to Puivert

Along the way

Camping Fontaulie-Sud
2 Chemin Trabenet
11500 Nébias
tel +33 4 68 20 17 62

Puivert

*Bonnes Saisons – Gîte & CH1 Route de l'Escale
Camsadourny
11230 Puivert
tel +33 4 68 20 75 07
tel +33 7 66 88 07 01
stay@bonnessaisons.com
www.bonnessaisons.com/stay

Relais des Marionnettes
19 Route Départementale
11230 Puivert
tel +33 4 68 20 80 69
www.gite-puivert.com

Camping Fontclaire
Campsadourny
Route de l'Escale
11230 Puivert
tel +33 4 68 20 00 58
www.campings11.fr

North variant

**Stage 4a: Cucugnan to
Camps-sur-L'Agly**

Camps-sur-L'Agly

Gîte d'étape & Camping La Ferme De
Camps
1 Rue du Château
11190 Camps sur l'Agly
tel +33 4 68 69 87 53
lafermedecamps@orange.fr
www.lafermedecamps.fr

Stage 5a: Camps-sur-L'Agly to Bugarach

Along the way

Gîte d'étape La Bastide (3km west of
Camps-sur-l'Agly, on the trail)
La Bastide
11190 Camps sur l'Agly
tel +33 4 68 69 87 57
cb@labastide.net

Bugarach

Chambre et table d'Hote le Presbytère
2 Rue du Presbytère
11190 Bugarach
tel +33 4 68 69 82 12
www.presbyterebugarach.fr/en

Gîte d'étape Maison de la Nature
Rue Cugurou
11190 Bugarach
tel +33 4 68 69 83
88maisondelanature@aol.com
www.maison-nature-rando.com

Stage 6a: Bugarach to Quillan

Quillan

*Hotel Cartier
Logis Hotel La Chaumière
31 Boulevard Charles de Gaulle
11500 Quillan
tel +33 4 68 20 05 14
H105@theoriginalshotels.com
www.theoriginalshotels.com/en

Gîte d'étape & Camping La Forge
(1km south of Quillan, off the trail)
Route de Perpignan
11500 Quillan
tel +33 4 68 20 23 79
laforge@ville-quillan.fr
www.laforgedequillan.fr

Chambres d'hôtes Le Petit Monde
5 Place de la République
11500 Quillan
tel +33 6 16 93 50 42

Camping La Sapinette
Avenue René Delpech
11500 Quillan
tel +33 4 68 20 13 52

Stage 7a: Quillan to Puivert

See accommodation listings for Stage 8.

Main route continued

Stage 9: Puivert to Espezel

Espezel

*Le 100 Unique
12 Grand Rue
11340 Espezel
tel +33 4 68 20 30 14
www.le-100unique.fr/en-fr

Stage 10: Espezel to Comus

Comus

Gîte d'étape de Comus – Chez Dine
et Lo
24 carrier de la glésia
11340 Comus
tel +33 4 68 20 33 69
www.gites-comus.com

L'Oustal Dé l'Annetta – Maison d'hôtes
1 Cami del Sarrat del Clot
11340 Comus
tel +33 4 68 74 81 26
www.loustaldelannetta.fr

Le Silence du Midi
1 Camí del Mouli
11340 Comus
tel +33 (0)468203626
info@lesilencedumidi.com
www.lesilencedumidi.com/en

Camurac (3km off trail)

Gîte d'étape La Marmite
11340 Camurac
tel +33 4 68 20 73 31
www.gites-camurac.fr

Camping Les Sapins
11340 Camurac
tel +33 4 68 20 38 11

Stage 11: Comus to Montségur

Montségur

Le Pelerin
111 Le Village Montségur
tel +33 5 34 14 00 39

Càmping de Montségur
Cap del Prat
09300 Montségur
tel +33 5 61 01 10 27

Chambres d'hôtes la Serre de Marou
(2km west of Montségur, near castle, on
the trail)
09300 Montferrier
tel +33 5 61 01 14 75

Les Ninouninettes
(4km along Stage 12, just off trail)
Hameau de Martinat
09300 Montferrier
tel +33 5 61 64 36 91
ninouninettes@yahoo.fr
www.les-ninouninettes.net

Stage 12: Montségur to Roquefixade

Roquefixade

*Gite d'étape
Le village
09300 Roquefixade
tel +33 5 34 14 04 48
contact@gite-etape-roquefixade.com
www.gite-etape-roquefixade.com

Gite d'étape à Roquefixade 'les
diligences'
Le village
09300 Roquefixade
tel +33 6 41 92 30 47

Stage 13: Roquefixade to Foix

Foix

*Hôtel Restaurant Lons
6, Place Georges Dutilh
09000 Foix
tel +33 5 34 09 28 00
hotel-lons-foix@wanadoo.fr
www.hotel-lons-foix.com

Le Leo de Foix
16 Rue Nöel Peyrevidal
09000 Foix
tel +33 5 61 65 09 04
contact@leodefoix.com
www.leodefoix.com

Camping du Lac
Labarre
09000 Foix
tel +33 5 61 65 11 58
www.vap-camping.fr

APPENDIX C
Useful contacts

Transport

Air

Booking sites

Skyscanner
www.skyscanner.net

Google Flights
www.google.co.uk/flights

Airports

Béziers Airport
www.beziers.aeroport.fr

Toulouse Airport
www.toulouse.aeroport.fr

Carcassonne Airport
www.aeroport-carcassonne.com

Perpignan Airport
www.aeroport-perpignan.com

Rail

Trainline
www.thetrainline.com

Eurostar
www.eurostar.com

SNCF train operator (Société nationale des chemins de fer français)
www.sncf.com

Train du Pays Cathare et du Fenouillèdes (Le Train Rouge): Fenouillèdes tourist train and railway
www.tpcf.fr

Coach

Omio
www.omio.co.uk

FlixBus
www.flixbus.co.uk

Bus

Limited local bus network
www.ledepartement66.fr

See SNCF website for rail replacement services

Local taxis

Taxis Cathare (Tuchan)
tel +33468454587

Taxi Claret (Saint-Paul-de-Fenouillet)
tel +33468592948

Allo Jacky (Quillan)
tel +33468200192

Taxi Jean-Michel (Lavelanet)
tel +33561013454

Taxi Deramond (Foix)
tel +33608991562

Tourism websites

France tourism website; search 'Languedoc' for relevant articles
www.us.france.fr/en

Aude area tourism
www.audetourisme.com

Occitan area
www.tourism-occitanie.co.uk

East Pyrenees tourism
www.les-pyrenees-orientales.com

North variant area
www.tourisme-limoux-in-aude.fr

Cathar dedicated site from Aude tourism
www.payscathare.org

More information about the Cathar
history in the region
www.cathar.info

Tourism information offices

Port-la-Nouvelle
1 Place Paul Valéry
11210 Port-la-Nouvelle
tel +33 4 68 48 14 81
www.visit-lanarbonnaise.com

Cucugnan
2 Route de Duilhac-sous-Peyrepertuse
11350 Cucugnan
tel +33 4 68 45 69 40
www.corbieresroussillontourisme.com
www.tourisme-corbieres-minervois.com

Saint-Paul-de-Fenouillet
(Closed weekends)
26 Boulevard de l'Agly
66220 Saint-Paul-de-Fenouillet
tel +33 4 68 59 07 57
www.st-paul66.com

Fenouillèdes area
21 Avenue Georges Pézières
66220 Saint-Paul de Fenouillet
tel +33 4 68 59 07 57
www.cc-aglyfenouilledes.fr

Quillan
(Closed Thursdays, Saturdays &
Sundays)
Square André Tricoire
11500 Quillan
tel +33 4 68 20 07 78
www.pyreneesaudoises.com

Axat
Rond point du Pont d'Aliès
11140 Axat
tel +33 4 68 20 59 61
www.pyreneesaudoises.com

Montségur
104 Le Village
9300 Montségur
www.montsegur.fr

Foix
29 Rue Theophile Delcasse
09000 Foix
tel +33 5 61 65 12 12
www.foix-tourisme.com

APPENDIX D
French–English glossary

French	English
auberge	small hotel usually offering food
Bons Hommes/Bonnes Femmes	the men and women ordained as Cathar 'Perfects', holy people
chambre d'hôte	guesthouse
chapitre	chapterhouse
chasse gardée	private hunting ground
col	mountain or hill pass
défilé	walkway or boulevard
église	church
épicerie	small grocery shop
faidit	a knight/lord from the south who has been dispossessed
fenêtre	window, in this instance somewhere with a view
garrigue	coastal scrubland
gîte d'étape	guesthouse
Grande Randonnée (GR)	network of long-distance paths in Europe
Langue d'Oc	historical dialect of Occitan
Langue d'Oïl	historical dialect of what is now Northern France
lavoir	wash house/open trough for laundry
mairie	town hall
maquis	French Resistance in WWII
pétanque	game of boules
pog	steep-sided rocky volcanic mound
puits	well
Sentier Cathare	Cathar Way
table d'hôte	a set menu at a fixed price, found in some accommodation
trains à grande vitesse (TGV)	high-speed trains

APPENDIX E

Further information and reading

Maps

Rando Éditions No.9 1:50,000 *Le Sentier Cathare* map

IGN (Institut Géographique National) 1:25,000 maps:

- 2547OT (Durban Corbières/Leucate)
- 2447OT (Tuchan)
- 2348ET (Prades/St-Paul-de-Fenouillet)
- 2347OT (Quillan)
- 2248ET (Axat/Quérigut/Gorges de l'Aude)
- 2247OT (Lavelanet)
- 2148ET (Ax-les-Thermes)
- 2147ET (Foix/Tarascon-sur-Ariège)

Guidebooks and literature

French Cathar Way guidebook: *Guide du Sentier Cathare*, 2011, Rando Éditions

Topoguides are the detailed French walking guides produced by the Fédération Française de la Randonnée Pédestre (FFRP), and although there isn't one for the Cathar Way, some do cover parts of the trail. They can be bought in the UK from Stanfords (www.stanfords.co.uk):

- *Sur le Traces des Cathares, Le Chemin des Bonshommes* (the GR107, ref: 1097)
- *Traversée de l'Aude Pays Cathare* (the GR36A, ref: 360)
- *L'Aude Pays Cathare* (ref: D011)
- *Le Pays de la Haute Vallée de l'Aude* (GR7A, ref: P112)
- *Le Pays Corbières Minervois* (ref: P116)
- *Traversée du Haut Languedoc* (ref: 716)

The Cathars

Lucien Bély, *The Cathars* (Éditions Sud Ouest, 2013)

Brian Catlos, *The Rough Guide to Languedoc and Roussillon* (Rough Guides, fifth edition, 2017)

Marcus Cowper, *Cathar Castles* (Osprey, 2012)

Emmanuel Le Roy Ladurie, Barbara Bray trans., *Montaillou* (Penguin, 2002)

Sean Martin, *The Cathars* (Pocket Essentials, latest edition 2014)

Kate Mosse, *Labyrinth* (Orion, 2005)

Stephen O'Shea, *The Perfect Heresy: The Life and Death of the Cathars* (Profile Books, 2001)

Linda Paterson, *The World of the Troubadours* (Cambridge University Press, 1993)

George Serrus, Roger Depledge trans, *The Land of the Cathars* (Editions Loubatières, 1990)

Janet Shirley trans. William Tudela & anon., *The Song of the Cathar Wars: A History of the Albigensian Crusade* (Routledge, 1996)

Jonathan Sumption, *The Albigensian Crusade* (Faber & Faber, 2011)

NOTES

NOTES

DOWNLOAD THE ROUTES IN GPX FORMAT

All the routes in this guide are available for download from:

www.cicerone.co.uk/1047/GPX

as standard format GPX files. You should be able to load them into most online GPX systems and mobile devices, whether GPS or smartphone. You may need to convert the file into your preferred format using a conversion programme such as gpsvisualizer.com or one of the many other such websites and programmes.

When you follow this link, you will be asked for your email address and where you purchased the guidebook, and have the option to subscribe to the Cicerone e-newsletter.

www.cicerone.co.uk

LISTING OF CICERONE GUIDES

The Cotswold Way
The Cotswold Way Map Booklet
The Great Stones Way
The Kennet and Avon Canal
The Lea Valley Walk
The North Downs Way
The North Downs Way Map Booklet
The Peddars Way and Norfolk
  Coast path
The Pilgrims' Way
The Ridgeway National Trail
The Ridgeway National Trail
  Map Booklet
The South Downs Way
The South Downs Way Map Booklet
The Thames Path
The Thames Path Map Booklet
The Two Moors Way
The Two Moors Way Map Booklet
Walking Hampshire's Test Way
Walking in Cornwall
Walking in Essex
Walking in Kent
Walking in London
Walking in Norfolk
Walking in the Chilterns
Walking in the Cotswolds
Walking in the Isles of Scilly
Walking in the New Forest
Walking in the North Wessex Downs
Walking on Dartmoor
Walking on Guernsey
Walking on Jersey
Walking on the Isle of Wight
Walking the Jurassic Coast
Walking the South West Coast Path
Walking the South West Coast Path
  Map Booklets:
  Vol 1: Minehead to St Ives
  Vol 2: St Ives to Plymouth
  Vol 3: Plymouth to Poole
Walks in the South Downs
  National Park

WALES AND WELSH BORDERS

Cycle Touring in Wales
Cycling Lon Las Cymru
Glyndwr's Way
Great Mountain Days in Snowdonia
Hillwalking in Shropshire
Hillwalking in Wales – Vols 1&2
Mountain Walking in Snowdonia
Offa's Dyke Path
Offa's Dyke Path Map Booklet
Ridges of Snowdonia
Scrambles in Snowdonia
Snowdonia: 30 Low-level and easy
  walks – North
Snowdonia: 30 Low-level and easy
  walks – South
The Cambrian Way

The Ceredigion and Snowdonia
  Coast Paths
The Pembrokeshire Coast Path
Pembrokeshire Coast Path
  Map Booklet
The Severn Way
The Snowdonia Way
The Wales Coast Path
The Wye Valley Walk
Walking in Carmarthenshire
Walking in Pembrokeshire
Walking in the Forest of Dean
Walking in the Wye Valley
Walking on Gower
Walking on the Brecon Beacons
Walking the Shropshire Way

INTERNATIONAL CHALLENGES, COLLECTIONS AND ACTIVITIES

Canyoning in the Alps
Europe's High Points

AFRICA

Kilimanjaro
The High Atlas
Walks and Scrambles in the
  Moroccan Anti-Atlas
Walking in the Drakensberg

ALPS CROSS-BORDER ROUTES

100 Hut Walks in the Alps
Alpine Ski Mountaineering
  Vol 1 – Western Alps
  Vol 2 – Central and Eastern Alps
Chamonix to Zermatt
The Karnischer Hohenweg
The Tour of the Bernina
Tour of Monte Rosa
Tour of the Matterhorn
Trail Running – Chamonix and the
  Mont Blanc region
Trekking in the Alps
Trekking in the Silvretta and
  Ratikon Alps
Trekking Munich to Venice
Trekking the Tour of Mont Blanc
Walking in the Alps

PYRENEES AND FRANCE/SPAIN CROSS-BORDER ROUTES

Shorter Treks in the Pyrenees
The GR10 Trail
The GR11 Trail
The Pyrenean Haute Route
The Pyrenees
Walks and Climbs in the Pyrenees

AUSTRIA

Innsbruck Mountain Adventures
The Adlerweg
Trekking in Austria's Hohe Tauern
Trekking in the Stubai Alps

Trekking in the Zillertal Alps
Walking in Austria
Walking in the Salzkammergut: the
  Austrian Lake District

EASTERN EUROPE

The Danube Cycleway Vol 2
The High Tatras
The Mountains of Romania
Walking in Bulgaria's National Parks
Walking in Hungary

FRANCE, BELGIUM AND LUXEMBOURG

Chamonix Mountain Adventures
Cycle Touring in France
Cycling London to Paris
Cycling the Canal de la Garonne
Cycling the Canal du Midi
Mont Blanc Walks
Mountain Adventures in
  the Maurienne
Short Treks on Corsica
The GR20 Corsica
The GR5 Trail
The GR5 Trail – Benelux and
  Lorraine
The GR5 Trail – Vosges and Jura
The Grand Traverse of the
  Massif Central
The Loire Cycle Route
The Moselle Cycle Route
The River Rhone Cycle Route
The Way of St James – Le Puy to the
  Pyrenees
Tour of the Queyras
Trekking in the Vanoise
Trekking the Cathar Way
Trekking the Robert Louis
  Stevenson Trail
Vanoise Ski Touring
Via Ferratas of the French Alps
Walking in Provence – East
Walking in Provence – West
Walking in the Ardennes
Walking in the Auvergne
Walking in the Briançonnais
Walking in the Dordogne
Walking in the Haute Savoie: North
Walking in the Haute Savoie: South
Walking on Corsica

GERMANY

Hiking and Cycling in the
  Black Forest
The Danube Cycleway Vol 1
The Rhine Cycle Route
The Westweg
Walking in the Bavarian Alps

For full information on all our guides,
books and eBooks,
visit our website:
www.cicerone.co.uk